Australian Stingless Bees
A Guide to Sugarbag Beekeeping

by John Klumpp

Earthling Enterprises
2007

Produced in co-operation with the
Australian Native Bee Research Centre (ANBRC)

© **2007, Earthling Enterprises Pty. Ltd.,**
    ABN: 81 050 5 919
    PO Box 5167, West End, Qld, Australia 4101
    Internet: www.earthling.com.au
    Email: info@earthling.com.au, and
    and John Klumpp

Reprinted: 2010, 2012, 2014, and from 2019 as print-on-demand

National Library of Australia Cataloguing-in-Publication

    Klumpp, John (John Douglas), 1948- .
      Australian stingless bees : a guide to sugarbag beekeeping.

    Includes index.
    ISBN 9780975713815 (pbk.).

    1. Bee culture - Australia. 2. Trigona - Australia. 3.
    Stingless bees - Australia. I. Title.

    638.12

Credits

The photos, unless otherwise specified, were supplied by, and are copyright to:
    © John Klumpp.
Other contributors, with thanks for their support, are each acknowledged in the caption, and include:

© Bob Luttrell	© Tim Heard
© Anne Dollin	© Carlos Vergara
© Lee Byrnes	© Carlos Alonso
© Marc Newman	© Lyndall Rosevear
© Frank Jordan	© Helen Schwencke
© Frank Adcock	© Bernhard Jacobi

Book production and publication:

Helen Schwencke for desktop publishing and production
Tim Heard, Anne Dollin, Frank Jordan and Helen Schwencke for editorial comment
Sue Wickenden and staff from Smartype for design support
Hanny Schwencke and Angus Fraser for proofreading

Cover illustrations:

Janet Hauser for front cover water colour painting of *Corymbia ptychocarpa* (Swamp Bloodwood).

Phillipa van Gilst for back cover painting, bee drawings on front cover, line drawings and other illustrations within the body of the book.

Photos on back cover by Bob Luttrell

Typesetting:

Text: NimbusRomanNo9, Heading: Arial, Header: InkFree, Captions: Liberation Serif

Australian Native Bee Research Centre (ANBRC)

Endorsement

Australian Stingless Bees by John Klumpp is a valuable handbook for anyone interested in keeping our native honeybees. These tiny native bees, fascinating for young and old, can be kept safely and easily throughout warm areas of Australia.

Written from the viewpoint of the native bee enthusiast, this detailed, easy-to-read book guides you through all aspects of the hobby – from understanding the inner workings of your nest to caring for your own stingless bee colony. It covers the basic beekeeping techniques used in Australia today, but also features John Klumpp's own unique designs for hives and hive accessories.

- Explore the behaviour, castes and life cycle of stingless bees;
- Learn how to find or buy a nest, transfer it into a box, and propagate it by the splitting or the eduction methods;
- Find out about all the hazards that might affect your hive; and
- Discover how to build a native bee friendly garden.

Beginners will enjoy John Klumpp's light-hearted and informal style, with its hearty dash of good Aussie humour. Yet this book is factual and informative enough to expand the knowledge of even experienced beekeepers.

John Klumpp is one of Australia's most creative and talented stingless bee keepers. His innovative designs have added a whole new dimension to the beekeeping techniques used in Australia's stingless bee industry.

Dr Anne Dollin
Australian Native Bee Research Centre
and the Aussie Bee Website: **www.aussiebee.com.au**
PO Box 74, North Richmond, NSW 2754

Dedication and Acknowledgements

Dedication

to Toni, Natalie & Debra
for time irrecoverable

Natalie, John, Toni and Debra

Acknowledgements

It would be a rare person indeed who could produce a publication of this nature without assistance and advice. I am certainly not such an individual and nor would I want to be because it would have meant missing out on the many friendships I have established, both near and far, in compiling the material for this book. I am not only grateful to all those who have generously given their time and shared their expertise to assist me but also to those pioneers of stingless beekeeping who paved the way for others like me to follow. If I do manage to raise the interest in stingless beekeeping just that little bit higher, then I want to acknowledge their efforts in providing a considerable platform to start with. They are too numerous to mention in full but I have attempted to record some below:

- Members of the scientific community for their painstaking research and the sharing of their expertise, especially: Dr Anne Dollin, Dr Tim Heard, Mr. Martyn Robinson, Prof Carlos Vergara (Mexico), Ms Ros Gloag, Mr Bernhard Jacobi (Germany) and Dr. Michael Batley.

- The ground breakers of stingless beekeeping with whom I had the opportunity to exchange ideas and information, including: Alan Beil (May 1949 – 14 August 2018. His friendship, his good humour and expertise in stingless beekeeping are sadly missed), Peter Davenport, Mark Grosskopf, Cec Heather, Bob Raabe, Bob Raymond, Alan Waters, Col Webb, and Russell Zabel.

- Helen Schwencke of Earthling Enterprises, my Publisher, who somehow found merit in my scribbling. Janet Hauser and Pippa van Gilst, the illustrators, whose art and meticulous attention to detail are both inspiring and astounding. Bob Luttrell, fellow beekeeper and photographer who is responsible for many quality photographs. Frank Jordan and Daphne Bowden for their encouragement and support.

- Finally, to my good mates Peter Scott and Greg Claussen whose friendship, patience and hands on assistance was invaluable.

Table of Contents

Name change for Trigona spp in Australia

Recent studies have proven the Australian stingless bees called *Trigona* in this book to be distantly related to the original *Trigona* of South America. Hence the genus name *Tetragonula* has been reinstated for Australia's species. We acknowledge this change, but have left the text of this book unaltered because the change has no other impact on the accuracy of the contents, and will have little impact on lay people wishing to keep or otherwise interact with these bees.

Foreword

On any sunny day throughout Australia bees can usually be found, just look for the nearest flowers. Bees are familiar to most people. Even the causal obervers in the cities and suburbs can identify at least one species of bee. Sadly what they usually refer to, recognise, or can point out, is the introduced European Honey bee (*Apis mellifera*). The 2000 or more species of Australian native bees go largely unrecognised and ignored by most people, except for a few entomologists, naturalists, and the Aboriginal people who live in the areas of Australia where the various bee species occur. Hopefully this book will help change this lack of recognition.

Many people find bees fascinating and their work ethic is an example used often enough in the classroom and work place to ensure that there is an interest in, and empathy for, the bees. Therefore, it wasn't too much of a surprise that, when Dr Anne Dollin & her husband Les founded the ANBRC (Australian Native Bee Research Centre) and launched the AussieBee magazine in 1997, it proved a great success. *Aussie Bee* was dedicated to providing information about Australian Native Bees and the research and findings about them. This was followed with information booklets on a variety of aspects of stingless social bee species and their culture, as information was discovered, swapped, and gathered from various other researchers both professional and amateur. The computer age soon caught up to this thirst for information on bees with two popular websites dedicated to Australian Native Bees (*Aussie Bee* and ANBees) having been launched, both with current research, new information and regular updates appearing frequently.

The majority of interest then, as now, was based around the little stingless social bees which are the only native bees which produce honey in a recognizable and harvestable form. This was well known to the indigenous Australians and was learned from them by some of the European colonists who adopted the anglicized name of Sugarbag Bees. The interest in how to keep these bees and the various attempts to harvest the honey, without destroying the colony which made it has, over the years, been the subject matter for many articles, papers and discussions. One of the pioneer contributors to a number of these articles was John Klumpp (Klumppy to those who know him) who even invented a new artificial hollow log hive design known as the KITH (Klumppy's Insulated Tubing Hive). His prolific findings, ideas, inventions, speculations and variations on a theme have been a great font of knowledge and a source of inspiration for many a stingless bee-keeper, both experienced and novice alike. Over the years several people have suggested he collate this scattered information into a book and this is what he has done here. It chronicles his own history of interest with these bees, his and other people's hive designs, methods, problems and solutions. It discusses how to find them, rescue them from fallen or doomed trees, and protect them from their many foes. There's even information on where to see some conveniently located nests of these bees and how to plant out a garden they will appreciate and all told in Klumppy's easily understood, often humorous and descriptive style.

This book will provide a wealth of tips and information brought together in a convenient form for all those interested in keeping the stingless or sugarbag bees. With increased knowledge comes greater appreciation and interest which, in turn, leads to more information being discovered and published. So take the plunge into the wonderful world of native bees, you never know what you'll find out or how deeply you'll become involved.

Martyn Robinson
Australian Museum

Prayer and Preamble

Ah Muzen Cab, the bee-god, can still be found today gazing with stony indifference from ancient Mayan temples. For thousands of years the Mayan's and their ancestors kept and revered the living symbol of this deity, the stingless bee Xunan Kab ("royal lady"). Today we know this bee, perhaps less romantically, as *Melipona beechii*. It is still widely kept in Central America, but regrettably its importance is on the decline due to changing beekeeping practices associated with the introduction of the honey bee from Europe and Africa.

Ah Muzen Cab, Mayan Bee God.
(Illustration by Phillipa van Gilst)

But stingless bees are not confined to The Americas; they occur throughout most of the tropical and sub-tropical parts of the world, including Australia. In many of these regions they occupied an important place in the culture of the native peoples, albeit without achieving the godlike status afforded to them by the Mayans. In most of those areas they were, and in some places still are, an important food source for the native peoples.

To the Australian Aboriginal people they were known by a variety of names including "Gilla" and "Sugarbag Bees". Although this latter expression is of European origin it now appears to be the most widely used term throughout Aboriginal communities. In some areas they are known as "sweat bees" due to their propensity for gathering salt from our perspiring bodies.

Not only was stingless bee honey highly prized by Aborigines as food, the bees' cerumen building material, a mixture of beeswax and tree resins, was also used for medicinal, ceremonial and everyday practical purposes.

A villager in Cuetzalan Mexico with his collection of **Scaptotrigona mexicana** *bees in terracotta pot hives. In Mexico, stingless beehives can be safely kept under the eaves of houses where they receive some protection from the weather. (Photo courtesy of Prof Carlos Vergara)*

The significance of stingless bees in Australian Aboriginal culture is depicted in a relief carving of a *Trigona carbonaria* bee that surmounts the arch of the Anthropology Department facing the Great Court at Queensland University's St Lucia campus. Carvings of other invertebrate animals that were prized as food accompany this image.

Even ancient cultures, and the time worn visage of Ah Muzen Cab himself, pale into insignificance when compared to the prehistoric lineage of stingless bees. They preceded humanity itself by an immense

The entry to the Anthropology Department at Queensland University's St Lucia campus as viewed from the Great Court. The insert shows in detail the relief carving of a stingless bee that surmounts this sandstone archway. Also depicted are other invertebrate animals that were important food sources for Australian Aboriginal people.

period of time. They were here long before the most primitive mammals evolved and shared the world with dinosaurs.

We know from fossil records that bees have existed for at least 80 million years. However certain features found in stingless bees fossilized in amber suggest that they may have been around much earlier than this, foraging in the primordial forests of cycads and conifers before the emergence of true flowering plants. When these put forth their first primitive blooms some 130 million years ago stingless bees may have adapted to be amongst their first pollinators.

Perhaps at no time in the past were the adaptive powers of these harmless little insects put to the test more than they are now, in today's rapidly changing world. In many places the effects of

These bees were trapped in tree resin millions of years ago and became fossilised as the resin turned to amber. They appear little different from the stingless bees we find in our gardens today. The whitish ring that surrounds the eye of the most prominent bee shown is believed to be trapped air or an impurity in the amber. (Photo courtesy of Bob Luttrell)

development, pesticides and even climate change are taking their toll. In Australian urban areas they are suffering from a lack of understanding about their very existence and their modest requirements for living.

However, these little creatures are survivors, and when their preferred home sites in hollow trees have been removed to make way for our preferred home sites in suburbia they will often find alternative places to live, such as in concrete block walls, meter boxes and in footpath service receptacles for telephone, electricity and water. Their colonies have even been found, perhaps somewhat unexpectedly, in tombstones and in discarded tyres. With their modest living requirements, left alone by us, they will happily carry on their industrious little lives in these places, collecting nectar and pollen from our azaleas, roses and citrus in place of the blue gums, iron barks and bloodwoods of natural settings.

The purpose of this book, therefore, is twofold. Firstly, to create an awareness and appreciation of our Australian stingless bees, and secondly, to provide practical advice on rescuing, keeping and propagating these fascinating little creatures.

I have written from the perspective of an enthusiast, or a hobbyist, if you like. While this status may provide me with a little license to include anecdotal information and narratives about personal experiences, along with the established knowledge, I am also conscious that the reader wants to be informed more than entertained in a publication of this nature. Trying to keep a foot in both camps is a balancing act at best. I trust that my readers will find that my footprint falls mainly on the informative side of the divide, but not to the extent that it stamps out the human elements of fascination and delight that should accompany an interest in bees that cannot sting you.

Above all, may my efforts not displease the Great Ah Muzen Cab and bring down upon me the usual sacrificial requirement of Mayan Gods.

Amen

1. Catching the Bug – a Personal Perspective

You have to be resilient to withstand the sympathetic glance or shake of the head when neighbours catch you out in the garden watching small black insects come and go from a hole in a log or box. When you try to explain that your hobby is keeping Australian stingless bees, the look often switches to scepticism, but it's true; there are bees that cannot sting and Australia is home to about a dozen species. They are known as stingless social bees and are not to be confused with the 1500 species or more of our native solitary bees - that can sting.

Inevitably the next question is 'do you get much honey from them?' I try to explain that while they do produce a lovely tangy bush honey, I don't keep them for that reason. I just enjoy having them around and propagating their hives. To forestall the return of the sympathetic glance I usually add that they are good pollinators, especially of trees such as macadamias. Perversely, I'd like to say 'you keep tropical fish don't you? How many fillets do you get?' but I doubt such a remark would assist me in promoting an interest in stingless bees.

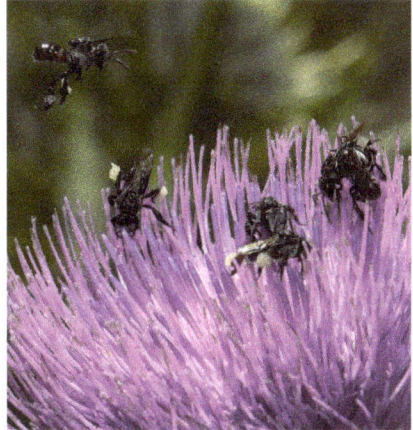

*Australia is home to about a dozen species of stingless social bees. Because of their small size the average gardener may not notice native bees such as these **Trigona carbonaria** foraging amongst their flowers. (Photo courtesy Bob Luttrell)*

My own interest in native bees goes back to my young childhood in the 1950's. Kids today would find it hard to believe that, apart from watching mum wrestle with the mangle on the newfangled washing machine, the only electronic entertainment available was the radio. We, therefore, spent a lot more time outdoors and generally took a greater interest in the natural world. Young people today would find it even harder to believe that many homes like ours did not have a telephone and of course mobile phones were a thing of fantasy in Dick Tracey comic books.

So when Mum made the regular trek to the nearest red PMG telephone box to make a call I would tag along. Leaning against the fence surrounding the yard of an old farmhouse nearby was a log containing a nest of stingless bees. Even as a child I knew what they were. I would sit quietly and watch them fly off and return with their little bundles of pollen or glistening resin until Mum thought she had had her fourpence worth of conversation, and we returned home.

My early interest in bees was maintained by keeping honey bees (*Apis mellifera*) for several years while living in the country. During this time my efforts to rescue the few stingless bee nests I came across, in sawmills and in firewood heaps, all failed. After

The absence of hollow trees in suburbia forces our stingless bees to find alternative accommodation – such as in this telephone service pit.

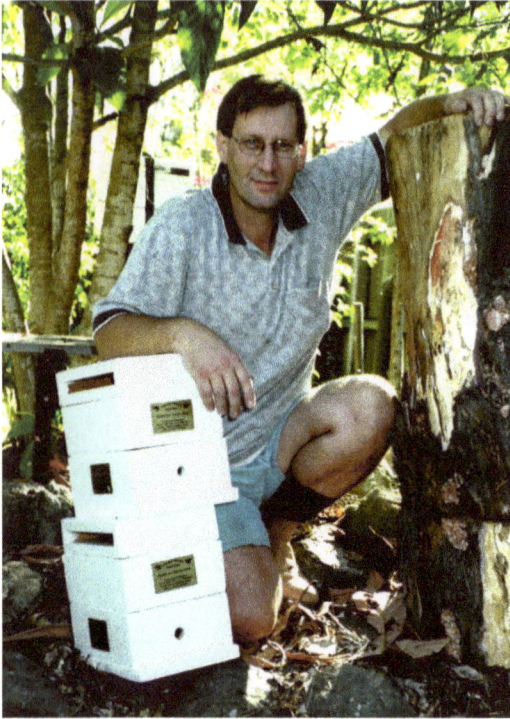

Russell Zabel, a well-known figure in the stingless bee field, has assisted mny others to get started in sugarbag beekeeping by providing them with quality hives and sound advice (Photo courtesy Anne Dollin).

Stingless bees are industrious little creatures. (Photo courtesy Bob Luttrell)

moving to a Brisbane bayside suburb with my wife, I parted company with the honey bees because of the potential problems they presented in this closely settled area.

Some years later, while travelling on the Warrego Highway, I became intrigued by a large ageing sign that stood outside a rural business at Hatton Vale. From memory this sign (which has since been refurbished) advertised: 'Zabels – Earthmoving, Tanks, Septic Tanks and Native Bees'. Fascinated as much by the diversity of the enterprise, as anything else, I decided to call in and eventually met up with Russell Zabel, one of the gurus of Stingless Beekeeping. The hive of *Trigona carbonaria* bees I subsequently bought from Russell, was delivered safe and sound a few days later by Australia Post. It was only later, through the excellent reference material published by Dr Anne Dollin of the Australian Native Bee Research Centre, that I was to learn that Australia has several species of native social bees and hundreds of species of solitary or semi-solitary bees.

What is there to enjoy in keeping stingless bees? I personally don't keep them for the honey they produce (although others do), and they are certainly not warm, cuddly animals devoted to, or dependent upon, human beings. On the contrary they are independent little creatures and their attitude towards us could best be described as complete indifference. On an individual basis they are small black insects with a passion for industry that has to be admired.

It is their communal nature that holds another part of the fascination I have for these bees. Social insects have developed over millions of years and, while their activities are no doubt instinctive, they give the impression of having collective intelligence. Who cannot marvel at the ability of these tiny creatures to travel far and wide in search of nectar and pollen, and yet be able to navigate back unerringly to a tree that looks very much like any other in the bush? They can also communicate with each other, not through speech, but through the use of pheromones or maybe in other ways we don't yet understand. Their behaviour offers so many opportunities for discovering new information. For example, how do they communicate the location of food since they don't do a honey bee dance?

Using a torch at night, and shining it through the glass observation panels on my hives, I have watched brood cells being constructed and provisioned by workers. I have also seen the queen make a fastidious inspection of their work before she lays a single egg and moves on, leaving the cell to be immediately sealed by a worker. I have observed their swarming behaviour and have propagated new hives by splitting old established hives and transferring eggs and larvae - all without the fear of being stung.

Another consideration is that stingless bees require virtually no care at all, so no provision has to be made for them when you go on holidays. You can have thousands of tiny industrious pets that don't yap, howl, screech or kill native birds and other animals. You don't have to worry about buying filters or heaters or changing their water and fishing them out when they turn up their toes. They won't bite the postman or sting the neighbour's kids and, of course, you don't need to feed them. They are fully self-sufficient, a delight to observe, and on top of that they pollinate your plants and may produce a little bit of tangy honey to drizzle over your ice-cream. If housed in an attractive artificial hive or a natural log, these little creatures also make an interesting garden feature.

A final attraction for me lies in the longevity of stingless bees. Not as individual bees, of course, but as a hive. Given just a little consideration and a hive made from durable materials the colony will outlast the dog, the cat, the budgie and you and me. The grandkids can argue over who will inherit granddad's native bee hive for their own back garden when he finally drops off the perch.

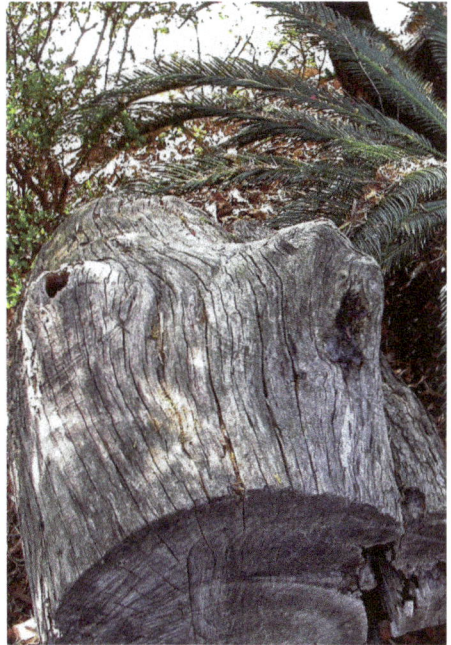

Stingless bee colonies, whether in artificial hives or natural logs, can make interesting garden features.

2. Bee Specific

*A **Trigona carbonaria** bee. The pattern ofthe fine white or grey hairs on the thorax can help to distinguish between the different Trigona species. (Photo courtesy Bob Luttrell)*

Now that we have had a whimsical introduction to Australian stingless beekeeping we need to get more specific.

Australia is home to approximately twelve species of stingless social bees, contained within two genera: *Trigona* and *Austroplebeia*. However, there is some uncertainty, particularly within the group Austroplebeia, as to whether some previously listed species are, in fact, separate species, or just strains, or variants caused by local environmental factors or isolation. Even in the more researched *Trigona* group, there has recently been a hitherto uncategorized species of bee added to the list of five established species (*T. carbonaria, T. hockingsi, T. mellipes, T. sapiens* and *T. clypearis*). This newcomer is called *Trigona davenporti* after Peter Davenport, a pioneer of stingless beekeeping who lives on Queensland's Gold Coast.

*Peter and Meg Davenport live on Queensland's Gold Coast and share an interest in stingless bees. Peter has had his pioneering efforts with stingless bees recognised by having a **Trigona** species named after him. (Photo courtesy Anne Dollin)*

If the taxonomists find species identification difficult, then it is doubly so for the amateur, especially when, to the unaided eye, all these bees appear as small black insects with pale faces (due to white or grey facial hair). They range in size from the tiny *Trigona clypearis* that has to stretch to make a length of 3.5mm, to *Trigona hockingsi* which, while still a diminutive 4.5mm long, is nevertheless our largest stingless bee. Under microscopic examination some distinguishing features become more obvious. For example, *Austroplebeia* bees have small yellow or cream body markings.

Austroplebeia australis bees showing the small cream coloured markings on the rear edge of the thorax that are a distinguishing feature of this species. (Left hand photo courtesy Bob Luttrell)

There are two common *Austroplebeia* species (*A. australis* and *A. symei*), but up to five more (*A. cockerelli, A. essingtoni, A. ornata, A. percincta* and *A. websteri*) are undergoing further assessment to determine their true status. Occasionally the type of hive entrance the bees construct can give a clue to their identity. Often it is necessary to open the hive to examine the brood structure and arrangement before a species can be positively categorised. No doubt DNA technology will make species identification easier in the near future for scientists, but I can't see the average amateur enthusiast having the necessary equipment to do this tucked away in the shed or spare room.

Austroplebeia australis bees don't deposit sticky resin around their entrance but, each evening, they construct a distinctive cerumen curtain across their doorway.

But not being able to positively identify each species should not diminish our enjoyment of keeping and propagating these social insects.

I keep three known species (*T. carbonaria, T. hockingsi* and *A. australis*) and possibly have a hive or two of *T. davenporti*, if the irregular brood comb is anything to go by.

While it may be difficult for a hobbyist to sort out the species in northern Australia, south of the Tropic of Capricorn three species predominate. There are only three recognised species. *Trigona carbonaria* is the most widespread of these. Natural hives have been found as far north as the Atherton Tableland in Queensland and as far south as Bega on the southern coast of New South Wales. They are the stingless bees most likely to be encountered in the south-east corner of Queensland and are still relatively common in the greater Brisbane area. Being the most tolerant of cooler temperatures, this is the species found naturally in the Sydney area and places further south. *Trigona hockingsi* does occur naturally as far south as Brisbane and nearby areas. *Austroplebeia australis* can also be found on the coast near Brisbane, but it is to the west of the ranges that this species comes into its own.

While positive species identification can be difficult and is beyond the scope of this publication, most enthusiasts will want to know, with some confidence, what type of bee inhabits the log in their backyard or is found in the surrounding bushland. Dr Anne Dollin is an acknowledged expert on Australia's native bees, and, through her facility, the Australian Native Bee Research Centre, produces both scientific and general publications on many aspects of Australia's bee fauna, including bee identification (see the Contacts and Resources section for information on how to access these resources).

Dr Anne Dollin with husband Les of the Australian Native Bee Research Centre. Since 1979 Anne and Les have worked together closely on their native bee endeavours and today are acknowledged experts in this field. Anne has produced a number of scientific papers as a result of their studies and several general publications on our Aussie bees that are available through the ANBRC. (Photo courtesy Anne & Les Dollin)

3. Bee Distinguished

*Three native **Trigona carbonaria** bees share a Camellia blossom with an introduced honey bee (**Apis mellifera**)*

We now know a little about the different species of Australian stingless bees but, apart from their small stature and the absence of a sting, what further characteristics distinguish them from other social bees such as the commercial honey bee?

Because the introduced honey bee (*Apis mellifera*) is such an important agricultural insect, most of us were taught about these creatures and their hives in our school years. It may further assist our understanding of stingless bees if we compare these two social species and consider their similarities and differences in some detail.

As there are several species of Australian stingless bees we will use *Trigona carbonaria*, arguably the most widely kept native bee, as the main model for our comparison with the introduced honey bee.

It appears that honey bees and stingless bees have followed a parallel evolutionary course in some respects, but have diverged significantly in others.

A feral honey bees' nest in a tree cavity showing the edge of one of the vertical combs comprised of many regular hexagonal cells made of beeswax.

Trigona hockingsi brood shows a less regular brood structure, in side view, than *Trigona carbonaria* (see opposite page)

Paradoxically, stingless bees have not always been stingless. Entomologists tell us that there are vestigial remains of a sting in their abdomens. It is interesting to contemplate why a social insect with such a powerful defensive weapon as a sting would lose that deterrent over time, especially when there is little evidence to suggest that other creatures were losing interest in robbing their sweet storehouse.

To put the differences between stingless bees and honey bees into perspective, perhaps we should first look at some of the similarities. The colonies of both types of bees consist of a single fertile queen, hundreds or thousands of female worker bees and a relatively small contingent of male bees (drones). Both the honey bee and stingless bee workers collect pollen as a protein source and nectar (which they convert to honey) as the energy food for the hive.

Hive structure

In natural settings both species seek out sheltered places, such as inside tree hollows, to build their nest. *Trigona carbonaria* bees wall off the living space they

Trigona carbonaria colony lifted out, virtually intact, from a storm damaged tree. (a) involucrum, (b) mature brood, (c) advancing front, partly realigned by the bees to cope with their new orientation after the tree had fallen, (d) pollen and honey pots, and (e) the batumen layers that sealed up both ends of the nest in the tree cavity.

*Stingless bees usually encase their brood inside an involucrum fashioned from thin layers of cerumen. Here the involucrum has been partly torn away during the rescue of this **Trigona carbonaria** colony revealing the regular flat spiral layers of brood inside typical of this species. (Photo courtesy Bob Luttrell).*

require with a thick layer of hard cerumen, often combined with other materials, which is known as the batumen. In a hollow tree the batumen is usually particularly solid above and below the colony to provide both a waterproof seal and protection from pests and invaders. Honey bees, perhaps because of their more robust nature and an effective deterrent in the form of a sting, do not build a solid defensive wall. However, they do use propolis, a substance that closely resembles cerumen in appearance, for sealing and securing parts of their hive structure.

Within all social bee nests there are structural components to accommodate three essential

*Inside a Mexican terracotta pot hive showing the horizontal brood comb built by **Scaptotrigona mexicana** bees. Stingless social bees do not arrange their brood in vertical combs like honey bees. (Photo courtesy Prof Carlos Vergara)*

elements for bee life – honey, pollen and the nursery where the eggs and young bees develop. We are all familiar with the shape of the honey bees' honeycomb. It is one of the architectural wonders of the insect world. Much less well known are the structures built by stingless bees. Evolution thrives on diversity and our native social bees have developed different, but equally effective, designs and methods for storing their food and raising their young.

Honey and pollen storage

Some of the differences become apparent in the hive's food storage methods. Honey bees store excess honey and pollen in regular hexagonal cells contained within vertical combs made of pure beeswax.

On the other hand, stingless bees hoard their excess stores in irregularly shaped pollen and honey pots which overlap and are attached to the walls and ceiling of their home. This makes the harvesting of stingless bee honey more difficult.

The honey pots, especially in the *Trigona* species, are constructed from a dark brown substance called cerumen which the bees produce by mixing wax from special glands in their bodies with tree resins collected by the foragers.

*While the interior of this **Austroplebeia australis** hive shows some signs of decay it depicts, very clearly, the difference between the dark brown honey pots at the top of the photo compared with the lighter coloured pollen pots in the foreground.*

*Two photographs of stingless bee brood showing the flat spiral pattern on the left which is indicative of **Trigona carbonaria** (photo courtesy Lyndall Rosevear) compared to the less regular structure of the closely related **Trigona hockingsi** on the right.*

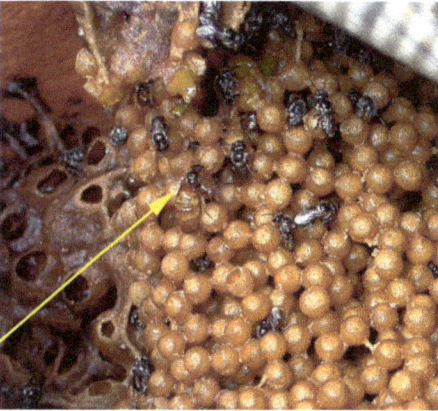

*These two photographs illustrate the spherical brood cells constructed by **Austroplebeia australis** and the 'higgledy piggledy' form of their brood mass. The queens are visible in both photographs. Note: the brood on the right is atypical in that it is a much darker colour than normal.*

Brood

With honey bees, the same type of hexagonal cell, utilized for honey and pollen storage, is also used to raise their next generation of worker bees, although young drones and queens (perhaps that should be princesses?) are allocated more spacious accommodation. The cells containing eggs and the subsequent stages of the developing bees are collectively known as 'brood'.

Stingless bee brood cells vary in both shape and arrangement from species to species and, in some cases, may be the only way of identifying a particular type of bee in the field. In all the species these brood cells are distinctly different from their storage cells. Their arrangement can extend from the regular broad spiral shape produced by *Trigona carbonaria* to the "higgledy-piggledy" pile of cells used by *Austroplebeia australis*. None of our stingless bee species arrange their brood in anything like the vertical combs used by honey bees.

*Another photograph of **Trigona carbonaria** brood. The larger cells (arrowed) on the outer edges of the brood mass are queen cells.*

Raising the next generation

It's in the bee nursery that the differences between honey bees and native stingless bees become more pronounced. To produce new workers, honey bee queens lay fertilized eggs in the bottom of empty normal cells. Nursery worker bees progressively feed the larvae that hatch out, starting with a special baby bee formula, sometimes known as 'bee milk'. It is not until the larvae develop to the stage where they are ready to pupate that the cells are finally sealed over. Eggs that are destined to become honey bee queens are laid in much larger cells and the emerging larvae are fed a special preparation called Royal Jelly.

Stingless bees employ a different technique to raise their young. Special brood cells are built that are both smaller and different in shape from the honey and pollen storage cells. These brood cells, the arrangement of which varies from species to species, are stocked with a mixture of honey, pollen and some glandular secretions produced by worker bees. The queen will lay an egg on top of this liquid food. The cell is then immediately sealed over by a worker bee. The larva that hatches out is left to develop and pupate on its own within the tiny cell. In most cases the queen will have chosen to lay a fertilised egg and this will develop into a worker bee. Drones are produced from unfertilised eggs in both honey bees and stingless bees by a process known as parthenogenesis.

With stingless bees, only the cells constructed for future queens are larger than the normal brood cells and, in the case of *Trigona carbonaria* bees, these are positioned on the outside of the brood spiral. However, they are provisioned and sealed in the same manner as for worker cells. It would appear that only the size of your meal determines whether or not you become a toiler or royalty in stingless bee society.

Hive Propagation

In honey bees, natural hive propagation is achieved by the old queen (having been trimmed down to her flying weight) accompanying a large swarm of workers to a new location. The swarming workers are engorged with honey, which they convert to wax for construction of comb at their new premises. Within the old hive, a virgin queen emerges, leaves temporarily for her mating flight and returns to the old hive to continue that colony. Beekeepers have modified this behaviour in honey bees in all manner of ways to ensure they maintain strong productive hives, and to avoid the loss of bees due to swarming.

Again stingless bee species do things differently. After her initial mating flight, the queen hangs up her flying goggles and helmet for good. She puts on too much weight to ever get airborne again. When a hive decides it wants to produce a new colony it will send out scout bees to find a suitable location. Worker bees will then visit that site over time to clean it up and prepare it for occupancy, eventually stocking the new place with some honey and pollen. This may take months or even longer in some cases. Eventually a virgin queen from the old hive arrives with her entourage to take up residency. Her mating flight occurs shortly afterwards, and egg laying soon follows. It is said the old colony maintains a supportive role towards its daughter colony, sharing workers for some time.

As their level of understanding of this behaviour grew the pioneers of stingless beekeeping began to devise ways of artificially housing and propagating these fascinating insects.

4. Colonial Life

This stingless bee hive, modelled on and early Australian bush hut, is one of many quaint hives designed and built by Darryl Bitossi.

The individual rights and freedoms of the masses (the female workers) are more than a little repressed in a stingless bee colony. Responding to pheromones and perhaps other chemical signals individual bees usually follow a fixed routine or react in a pre-programmed way to danger and other stimuli throughout their lives.

If I were to deal with the subject of an individual worker bee's life simplistically, her eulogy would take just a few words. Approximately fifty days after her mother, the queen, laid an egg she emerged from her brood cell as a young adult bee (known as a callow). In her youth she worked hard on various indoor duties and while foraging during her twilight days managed to avoid all the predators outside. She died on the evening of her fiftieth day surrounded by five thousand sisters. The next day her earthly remains were deposited on the lawn in front of the hive by one of her sisters in a quiet ceremony without mourners.

As sad as I may have made this sound, the loss of a single worker bee that has fulfilled her life's purpose is of little or no consequence to the colony. The colony has a life of its own on a different dimension and at its heart is the brood mass. Ultimately it is the slow and regular cycle that occurs within this brood mass that governs the life of the colony. Understanding this rhythm has enabled stingless beekeepers to refine their propagation techniques and thereby improve their success rate, so it is appropriate to look at this aspect of the colony's life in more detail.

Unlike the various strains of honey bees, most species of Australian stingless bees have received relatively little scientific attention. While much of what follows will have general application to all our stingless bees, the information presented here (and throughout the publication) is largely based on the current knowledge and understanding of the more widely kept species, namely: *Trigona carbonaria*, *Trigona hockingsi* and *Austroplebeia australis*.

As a rule the brood is positioned towards the centre of the nest structure where it can be better protected. It is usually, but not always, encased in multiple protective layers of thin cerumen fashioned into various chambers and passageways. This structure is called the involucrum and is thought to insulate the brood and perhaps allow control of the ventilation and humidity.

This area is also the queen's domain and she will wander, seemingly at random, over the sealed cells until it becomes time for her to fulfil her reproductive duties. The egg-laying process is quite a ceremony to watch in itself, especially in Trigona sp. bees. A small group of workers takes some time to construct a neat little cell out of cerumen. It is smoothed and polished on the inside before it is provisioned by a relay of workers, each carrying one tiny drop of liquid food. The queen then approaches and is sometimes buffeted towards the cell by a gauntlet of the cell builders. From my observations, rarely will the initial cell-provisioning meet with her approval, so workers will be despatched to bring more provisions until finally everything receives her royal assent.

The egg is laid in a brief second and immediately afterwards one of the worker bees inserts the tip of her abdomen into the cell and by working round and round somehow manages to produce a neat convex cap over the cell. As most living and growing things need oxygen, I suspect that either a pocket of air is trapped beneath this cap or it is porous to allow the passage of air to the larva as it develops.

It is for this reason that most beekeepers caution against inverting a hive when transporting or installing it. The concern is that the brood cell's liquid contents will block the airflow through the porous cap resulting in the suffocation of the larva within. However, some of the ancient practices still followed by Mexican stingless beekeepers which recently came to light cast doubt on this premise.

While it is appropriate to examine the development of a single brood cell in the above context we must keep in mind that these cells are not usually built in isolation.

In a strong hive several cell-building teams will be at work constructing cells in batches on the brood mass, the general shape of which may be peculiar to that species of bee. In *Trigona carbonaria* this is in the regular form of a broad flat horizontal spiral; not unlike a somewhat flattened version of the three dimensional structure scientists construct to represent the basic building block of all life on this planet – the DNA molecule.

Whether we are dealing with *Trigona carbonaria* bees with their regular brood spiral or the less tidy arrangement of cells typical of *Austroplebeia australis* the cell builders keep adding new cells, steadily extending the brood mass. These new cells are known collectively as the 'advancing front', but being confined within a hive the bees can only continue to advance the front so far, right? Well, this is where the really clever bit comes in.

The advancing front of **Trigona carbonaria** *is comprised of the newest brood cells and moves steadily upwards. (Photo courtesy Lyndall Rosevear)*

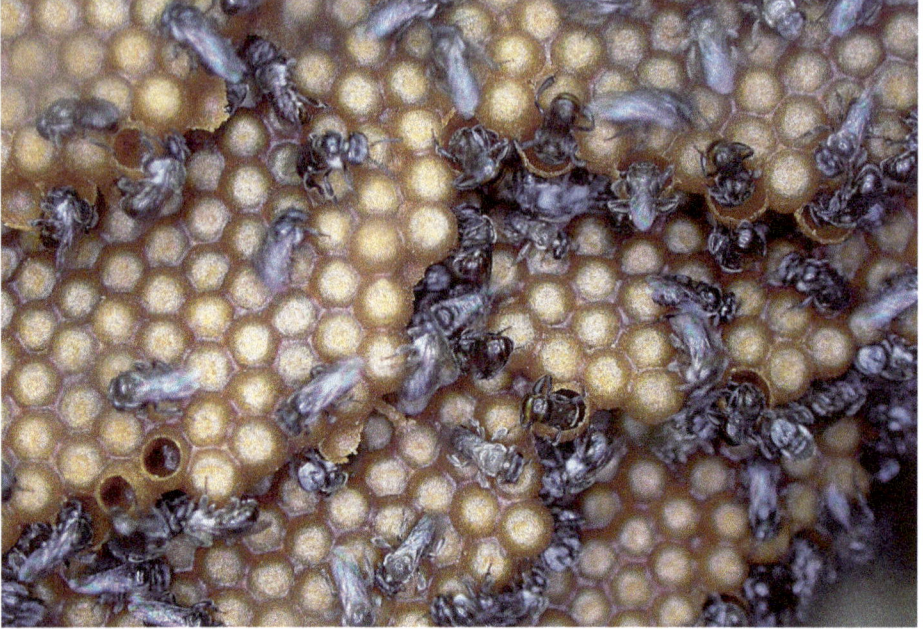

Trigona carbonaria brood cell builders at work.

By the time the cell builders at the top reach the upper limit of the cavity inside the involucrum, the cells at the bottom begin hatching out, leaving an ever increasing space down below. The workers from the penthouse level drop down to the basement to continue the advancing front down there. This cycle can go on indefinitely.

The position of the advancing front is important to the beekeeper who is contemplating hive propagation by either the splitting or eduction methods, which are dealt with in detail in later sections.

After hatching, the tiny larva grows slowly as it consumes the food around it. Eventually no food is left but, by this stage, the larva has grown to the point where it fills the cell. Now is the time for it to spin a silken cocoon around itself within the cell in order to pupate.

*The grub-like **Austroplebeia australis** larva (left) goes through an amazing transformation during pupation before becoming an adult bee. The larva and the two partly developed bees (right) were unfortunate in being dislodged from their sealed wax cells during a hive rescue.*

Somehow the worker bees know when the larva has pupated, and they will then proceed to strip away the cerumen above and below the cocoon for re-use on new brood cells. As the brownish cerumen is removed the lighter coloured cocoons are exposed, thereby revealing to the beekeeper the areas of mature brood. If you examine this older brood even more closely you may notice two small indistinct dark spots on the top of each cell. These are the eyes of the imagos (fully formed young bees almost ready to emerge) seen through the semi-transparent cocoon.

When the new bee finally emerges all that is left of the brood cell is the empty pupa casing and within that the larva's faecal pellet. These elements can't be recycled, so a worker bee bundles it all up tightly and dumps it some distance from the hive.

*The older brood – the eyes of the soon to emerge **Austroplebeia australis** bees can just be seen through their cocoons now that most of the cerumen has been stripped away by worker bees. In the foreground is a mature queen cell and in front of that four young brood cells still encased in cerumen for comparison.*

*Left: these **Austroplebeia australis** bees have stored old pupae cases in the corner of this display hive for later disposal. Right: **Trigona carbonaria** bee carrying out old pupae cases on the first fine day after bad weather.*

However, if weather conditions are bad, or if the bees are otherwise occupied, they will store these old cocoons in a rubbish heap, usually just inside the hive entrance, for later disposal.

It is believed that stingless bee drones, because they are raised in the same sized cells as the workers, take about the same time to develop into adult bees. However, larvae destined to become future queens appear to take a few days longer to emerge from their larger quarters.

These two photos show recently emerged worker bees (called callows) that are noticeably lighter in colour than older bees in the nest. Despite their tender age they have an important role to play in the colony.

5. Caste Distinction

We have seen how the three different castes of bees fit into the social structure of the colony and the role each plays in the life cycle of the hive. I hesitated before using the term 'life cycle' in this context as the usual connotation refers to the birth, growth, reproduction and then death of an individual creature, whereas the life span of a hive organism is not so clearly defined. The individual bees are born to die like all mortal things, but during their brief lives the vast majority of bees (the female workers) forego reproduction, or at least are suppressed in this regard and instead devote their energies to raising the offspring of their royal mother or sister.

This anomaly in one of the usual driving forces of nature troubled great minds like Darwin's when composing his ideas on evolutionary forces. While the conundrum has now been scientifically explained, it still stands as testimony to the wonderful diversity and complexity of nature on our planet. But enough amateur philosophising, we don't need to understand all the complex theories of kinship in social insects to keep and propagate stingless beehives. That said, it is important to be able to distinguish between the different castes that arise within a colony from this arrangement, so perhaps we should look at each one in more detail.

The Fertile Queen

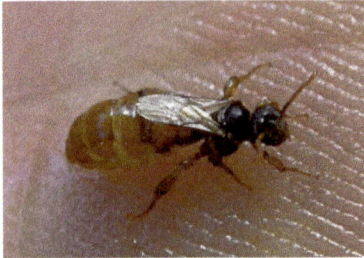

*A mature **Trigona carbonaria** queen disturbed from her egg-laying duties. (Photo courtesy Bob Luttrell)*

A stingless bee queen mates only once on a nuptial flight, during which it is believed she flies strongly upwards to a considerable height, leaving all but the strongest drone in her wake. After mating, she abandons her prince consort to his fate and returns to the colony to begin her egg-laying career. Sperm from this single mating is stored within a special organ in the queen's body called a spermatheca, and can be released by her as required to produce all the fertilized eggs laid during her reign. She may be either displacing an old tired queen in a long established colony that decided to re-queen, or instead starting off a new hive somewhere else with a retinue of workers; unlike the honey bee queen she will never fly again. In Australian stingless bees the queen is approximately twice the size of a worker to start with, but after mating the size difference becomes even more noticeable as her abdomen expands with eggs. The tissues connecting the segments of her abdomen stretch enormously, and being translucent give her abdomen a distinctive brown and cream appearance. A mature laying queen is easily distinguished from any other bee in the colony.

Virgin Queens

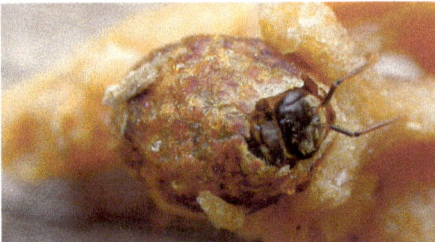

*A young **Austroplebeia australis** queen emerges from her brood cell (left) to face an uncertain future.*

While not strictly a separate 'caste', these unmated queens form a very small, but nevertheless important, component of the hive. They are the colony's insurance policy against the loss of the fertile queen. It is believed that well established colonies produce these 'princesses' more or less continuously. Some are allowed to survive for a while after hatching but if not called upon to replace the old queen or to found a new colony they are killed by either the workers or by the primary queen. In some overseas species of stingless bees, these virgin queens are housed in special cerumen chambers constructed by the workers. There they remain until they are called upon

A newly emerged **Trigona carbonaria** *virgin queen*

either for royal duties, or for an unceremonious end. While awaiting their fate they are provided with room service by the workers. In other species a virgin queen is ringed by a contingent of workers that accompany her wherever she goes within the hive.

While it appears that Australia's stingless bees also retain virgin queens within the colony structure, there is currently no information available on how long they are tolerated or whether or not they are constantly escorted by a cordon of workers. It seems unlikely that our bees build special quarters to house these young royals because none have been found (or at least reported) during hive splitting or other invasive operations. However, there is still a lot to be learned about this aspect of colony life. This is yet another area where observation by beekeepers may help to fill some of the gaps in our current knowledge.

Workers

Trigona carbonaria worker bees are well equipped to collect food for the colony. Nectar is transported in an internal honey sac while pollen is loaded into the corbiculae (pollen baskets) on the rear legs. The last photo shows a worker that has encountered a flower rich in pollen that is now daubed over various parts of her body. She will comb this into two neat little balls before commencing her return journey to the hive. (Centre and right hand photos courtesy Bob Luttrell)

In the matriarchal world of social bees, sterile females overwhelmingly dominate the population. These are the worker bees. They are destined by chance and an iniquitous outcome of evolution, to fulfil a more menial role than their mother, the queen, or their royal sisters. Both workers and queens develop from fertilised eggs, but the smaller brood cells provided for workers and the consequential restriction of rations not only limits their size, but also their fertility. There are exceptions to this rule. Workers, while they cannot mate, do have the capacity to lay eggs under certain circumstances. They are usually constrained from doing so by the effects of pheromones released by the fertile queen. Worker eggs, being unfertilised, can only develop into drones. In Australian species laying workers become noticeable only when a hive becomes queenless for some reason and the social order of the colony is breaking down.

I am of course being a little facetious in implying that workers are starved during their embryonic development, which leaves them as stunted individuals only suited to a life of drudgery. Nature is indifferent to our notions of fairness, and millions of years of evolution have determined that this creature's survival is best served by a social system where the castes may have different characteristics, but each performs an essential function. Workers develop fully for their particular role and are well equipped for the tasks they have to perform. They have special glands to produce wax, which emerges as tiny flakes from between their abdominal segments. They also have glands in their mouths to make secretions that are added to honey and pollen to produce baby bee food, and yet others to produce pheromones to leave scent trails and other important hive signals. Their rear legs have evolved to incorporate a shallow basket-like structure (known as a corbicula) that is ideal for transporting pollen and glistening drops of tree resin.

Newly emerged worker bees, known as callows, are noticeable as they are lighter in colour. Despite their tender age they are immediately called upon to begin work in the heavy industry section. Combining their wax with plant resins brought in by returning foragers produces the cerumen necessary for all forms of hive construction. However, the ability to make wax declines with age and, in time, they will move on to perform other functions in the hive, such as rubbish disposal and guard duties. Finally, in their twilight days they will join the hive's foraging force.

Workers make up such a large proportion of the colony's numbers that it is probably easier to distinguish them by describing the physical characteristics of the other castes.

Drones

Male bees or drones develop from unfertilised eggs laid by the queen, and less commonly by a worker, through a process known as parthenogenesis.

Before we go on to the distinctive physical features of drones, perhaps we need to put our minds in gear and consider the interesting conundrum that parthenogenesis presents to

Drones may congregate in large numbers on thin twigs and branches in the late afternoon and remain in these clusters throughout the night.

family (genetic) relationships within the bee colony. It means that no drone bee has a father - he only has a grandfather! Furthermore, the female bees (including young queens) emerging from adjoining cells from eggs laid by his mother are not his full sisters because they developed from eggs fertilised by a drone that couldn't have been his grandfather. Now that you've digested all that you are probably wondering what practical relevance it has to us as beekeepers. Well, none really, except that it may serve to highlight that when we leave the realm of higher animals and enter the wondrous world of social insects we need to reassess our ideas about reproduction and genealogy.

Unlike honey bees, stingless bees don't appear to construct special brood cells to raise male bees. The queen alone is left to determine the number of drones the colony should produce by regulating how many unfertilised eggs she lays in worker sized brood cells. Not surprisingly, the drones that emerge from these cells are the same size as workers, which makes them difficult to distinguish on an individual basis with the naked eye. However, collectively they can usually be identified outside the hive by an experienced beekeeper when they form up into a loose swarm and take up station near a hive. Often this will be in an area of full or dappled sunlight. Perhaps they just like to cruise around in the warm sunshine while waiting for some 'action' in the form of an emerging virgin queen. Sometimes they will camp out at night by clustering on small twigs on the outermost branches of nearby bushes.

When you get up close and personal with the aid of a magnifier or microscope, the differences between drones and workers become more apparent. The drones don't do any foraging so while their hind legs superficially resemble those of workers, a close inspection will reveal the absence of pollen baskets. Their sense organs need to be top rate to detect the presence of a young queen amongst all the workers and to follow her on a mating flight. As a result their antennae are longer than those of the workers; in fact they have thirteen segments compared to the workers' twelve. For you technically-minded types these counts include the scape and pedicel with the flagellum. The drone's compound eyes are also larger than those of the worker and, when combined with the male's smaller mandibles, it gives his 'face' a more wedge shaped appearance.

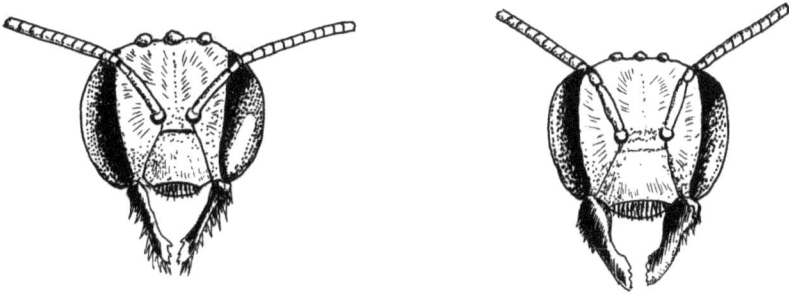

The face of a **Trigona carbonaria** drone (male) on the left compared with a worker (female) of the same species. The larger eyes and smaller mandibles of the male together with his longer antennae are distinguishing features. (Illustrations by Phillipa van Gilst)

Finally, there are the distinctive male genitalia at the tip of the abdomen as shown in the accompanying illustration. This may not be fully extended in all captured specimens, but is usually visible to some degree under reasonable magnification. Complex reproductive organs seem to be common amongst insects, but perhaps because the stingless bee queen only has one opportunity to mate in her life the drone must be very specially equipped to ensure a successful outcome for the colony.

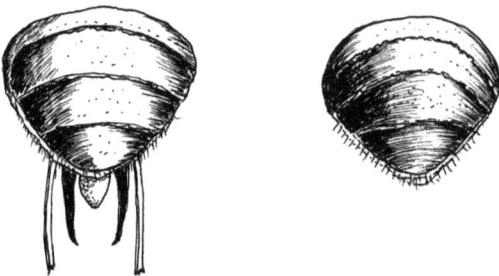

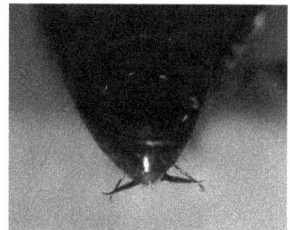

This close up picture shows the complex reproductive organ of the **Trigona carbonaria** drone fully extended.

These illustrations show the drone's abdomen (left) compared with the worker's (right). (Illustrations by Phillipa van Gilst)

6. The How, When, Where and Why of Finding Stingless Bee Colonies in Bushland

*You will find yourself looking for native bees wherever you are. This **Trigona carbonaria** nest is one of two in a Camphor Laurel tree close to the Brisbane CBD*

Why?

Well, once you have been bitten by 'the bug', you will find yourself looking for stingless bee colonies whenever you visit a suitable patch of bushland. You may be out bushwalking, visiting a National Park, or just breaking a long drive by a stop at a roadside rest area, when you'll catch yourself scanning the trees for suitable hollows and looking for the tell-tale signs of native bees.

You may want to save colonies from an area of bushland about to be levelled for the latest shopping centre or housing development, or to obtain a nest from trees that have already been felled and have been stacked up for burning. The pace of urban development around coastal towns and cities is such that there are usually plenty of opportunities to rescue colonies from destruction. But, even in rural areas, tracks of bushland are constantly being cleared for roadways, fence lines and, in some situations, for farming. Nests in trees felled by storms or bushfires may also need saving, especially if the tree has been badly damaged in the fall.

*These two photos show a **Trigona carbonaria** nest exposed by storm damage. On the left the rescuer is indicating the location of the nest's entrance.*

Given these opportunities, it should be unnecessary to fell trees in natural areas that are not under threat of development to obtain a colony of stingless bees. Hollow trees are natural apartment blocks in our bushland, whether they are living or dead. They are home to all manner of creatures and the felling of each one depletes and degrades our natural heritage just that little bit more.

Whether your motive is hive rescue, or you just want to observe colonies in their natural state, the first step is to find them – and that's not as easy as you might think. A friend of mine has lived on an acreage property near Brisbane for over 25 years. Not long ago he became interested in stingless bees and started searching for wild colonies. He found the first one in his own backyard less than a metre off the ground in an old tree he had passed every second day. Judging by the amount of resin that had accumulated around the entrance, the colony had been in residence on the property longer than he had.

I've been told that one method the Aborigines used to find a stingless bee's nest was to catch a foraging bee on a flower and to attach a small piece of feather to one of its rear legs. It would then be released and watched in flight until it arrived back at the colony. Unfortunately my fingers are too big and clumsy for me to even contemplate such a dexterous exercise and my eyes are probably not up to the task of tracking the bee in flight, even if I could. However, there are other ways the reasonably observant person can locate a colony so we'll explore those in more detail, but first we need to look at some other factors.

*Judging by the amount of resin around the entrance this **Trigona carbonaria** colony has been established for quite some time.*

Where?

You're likely to find stingless bees anywhere in their natural range where there are mature trees with suitable hollows - trees inhabited by termites are well worth a look. With their insatiable appetite for cellulose, the termites may have created a number of suitable cavities for bees. Termites often disclose their presence by building meandering covered walkways up the tree's trunk to protect themselves from sunlight and predators. Often their nest will also be visible at some point along the trunk or on one of the major branches.

Don't ignore fallen trees when looking for stingless bees, even those that have been on the ground for years. In many cases a colony will survive the fall and, given half a chance and a little time, will reestablish itself in its new orientation.

Provided their homesite is about the right size, our little bees don't seem to care about the quality or origin of the woodwork around them. They can be found in nearly any type of tree, ranging from the sparse weather-beaten Ironbark up on the stony ridge to the luxuriant introduced Camphor Laurel down by the creek. And, of course, the bees don't confine themselves just to trees. Some of the stingless bees that inhabit the natural bushland areas of our far north are just as likely to be found in rock crevices. Even the more widespread *Trigona carbonaria* can have diverse tastes in housing when tree hollows are in short supply.

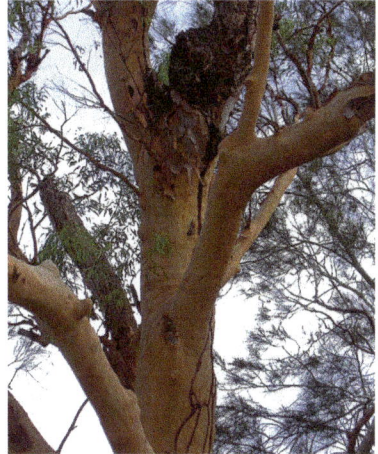

Termites are the home builders for many of our native creatures. In this tree the main termite nest is situated high up on the trunk, but also visible are the meandering covered pathways they build out from the main structure.

Occasionally you will find a stingless bee or two ensnared in a spider's web.

*This area of bushland is home to a number of stingless bee colonies. The dead fire scorched tree in the foreground houses a colony of **Trigona carbonaria**.*

*Fresh Grass Tree (**Xanthorrhoea** sp.) flower spikes are especially attractive to stingless bees.*

When?

The time of the year isn't all that important but, as we've discussed before, even our most cold tolerant social bees (*Trigona carbonaria*) won't get out of bed until the temperature reaches 18 degrees centigrade, and will usually wait until it's a few degrees higher again, before they get fully motivated to forage. So pick a warm, calm day and equip yourself properly for the hunt. Besides your wide brimmed hat, sunglasses, sunscreen, walking boots, water and notebook, consider carrying a pair of binoculars and a plastic sheet or clean hessian bag. Just a word of caution though: these weather conditions also rouse some of our other bushland denizens from their usual lethargy. So while you're wandering about scanning the trees for signs of bees just keep an eye on the track in front of you for any of those wriggly sticks that might be about.

Before we move onto the all-important 'how' (to find the colony of stingless bees), perhaps we should first look around the bushland to see if there are any obvious signs of them in the vicinity. Look at cobwebs as you wander about. These are not a particularly reliable indicator of the presence of stingless bees, but occasionally you will see a bee or two ensnared by a spider. More importantly, check out any flowering plants. Some plants are better drawcards than others. I find Grass Tree (*Xanthorrhoea* spp.) flower spikes particularly reliable. If the spike is bearing fresh flowers covered with bush insects and no stingless bees are in attendance then, in my experience, you are wasting your time looking for bees in that area. However, more often than not, they will be foraging there in force and you can start your search with confidence, knowing that within a radius of about 500 metres there is at least one stingless bee colony.

How?

It takes most people some time and practice to learn the knack of finding a colony of stingless bees in natural bushland. It's not that they hide from us or are even particularly well camouflaged; it's just that they are indistinct. Tiny black insects entering or leaving a small hole in a hollow tree can be easily missed by a casual inspection. So the first lesson to be learned is to give every likely looking tree a thorough going over. Start at the very bottom and work slowly upwards, sometimes hives are found within inches of ground level. *Trigona carbonaria* bees usually plaster the area around their entrance with sticky tree resins possibly as a defence against ants and other invaders. This can appear as a dark or even shiny patch on the bark of the tree depending upon the angle of the light. So check out any such spots on the trunk or major branches of the tree.

Another giveaway (if the light is coming from the right direction) is the glistening wings of the foraging bees as they enter and leave their colony on a direct course in or out. Often there will be a number of other small insects flying around, their wings glistening in the warm sunshine as well, but they've never heard about making a beeline for anything and just wander aimlessly about. So only follow those back to the tree that seem to have a purpose in life.

Still can't find the nest? Move in close to the tree and, shielding your eyes from the sun, look upwards along the line of the trunk. If the trunk and major branches can be positioned against a background of white cloud so much the better. Again, check for small black insects coming and going on a mission, but also look for any larger insects hovering in the one spot for any length of time. Bembix wasps, insects just a little smaller than a honey bee, position themselves in front of stingless bee colonies in summer.

These wasps pick off some of the foraging bees to feed their offspring, which are housed in tunnels that the adult wasps dig in nearby sandy soils. They are a reasonably reliable pointer to the entrance of a stingless beehive. Another indicator can be the presence of a syrphid fly. These flies do not hover like the Bembix wasps, but have a distinctive appearance. They are a wasp mimic, sporting the bright yellow and dark brown livery of a medium sized wasp or hornet, but lacking their stinger. Unusual antennae that appear to branch from a single stem are an identifying feature. Female syrphid flies lay their eggs adjacent to the hive and their larvae emerge to feed on the colony's honey and pollen stores. But more of this later, in the section "The Good, the Bad and the Ugly".

Trigona carbonaria bees usually plaster the area around their entrance with sticky tree resins whereas other stingless bees species don't.

Bembix spp. wasps can often be seen hovering in front of stingless beehives in the summer months. (Photo courtesy Bob Luttrell)

The syrphid fly is a very effective wasp mimic, but it has no sting.

Now bring the binoculars into play and check out every likely looking nook and cranny in the upper branches. If, like me, extending your head backwards repeatedly in this manner literally gives you a pain in the neck, then lay your piece of plastic or hessian bag in the shade, lie down and scan the tree at your leisure. You've found one, that's great, but keep looking. Up to five stingless bees' nests have been located in the one tree. If you've had no luck move on to the next likely looking tree, remembering to check out any flowering plants or cobwebs on the way.

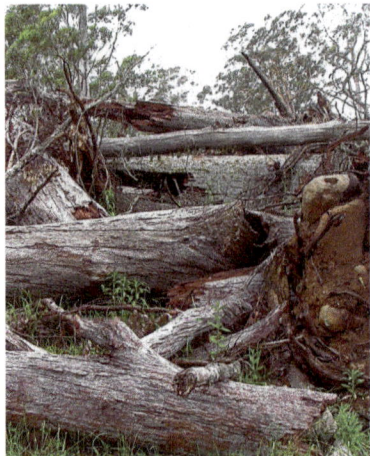

Stingless bee colonies can sometimes be found in trees that have been bulldozed into piles for burning.

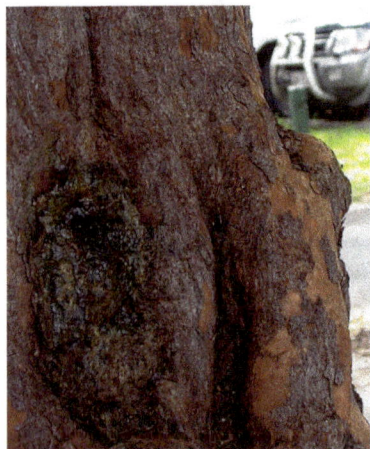

This **Trigona carbonaria** colony has lived for more than 20 years in the base of this tree at the entrance to a ferry terminal carpark in an inner Brisbane suburb.

When you've found a colony mark down its location in your notebook carefully so that you can check on its progress next time you're in the vicinity. A small GPS unit can be extremely useful in this regard, especially if you are mapping all the nests in an area destined to be clear felled for development and you want to come back and rescue them at a later date.

Finding colonies in fallen trees, especially those that have been bulldozed into piles for burning, can be a slightly more difficult exercise. Stand at the end of the pile and look along it towards a plain surface, such as the sky or white clouds. You may have to get down low to do this depending on the lie of the land. Bembix wasps may still be in attendance if there is a nest present, but you are more likely to spot syrphid flies as they target stingless bee colonies that have been disturbed or damaged. Provided the weather is warm enough, early mornings or late afternoons may be more productive than a midday search. Often the bees' glistening wings are more visible when the sun is closer to the horizon.

Be careful poking around in timber piles. Sometimes large trees can be dislodged quite easily and unexpectedly with serious results to anyone clambering over them. Snakes may also be about, looking for an easy feed of dislodged animals in these heaps so proceed around them cautiously. Needless to say, you should obtain appropriate approval before inspecting the area or removing colonies from private property.

To get you started with your bee hunting I have included a 'Register of Stingless Beehives in Public Places' at Appendix 1. This is a list of known stingless bee colonies in places anyone can access. A number of these locations are in suburbia and at least two are quite close to Brisbane's Central Business District.

The Register, which appears on the Australian Native Bees website http://www.australiannativebees.com/, has been designed to allow native bee enthusiasts to monitor hives over time.

7. Logs, Boxes and Other Abodes

This quaint minature cottage hive was donated, by Darryl Bitossi, to the Redlands IndigiScapes Environmental Centre at Capalaba for display purposes.

The favourite home site for most species of our stingless bees is a hollow tree, be it living or dead. However, they are not all that finicky and, particularly in suburbia where hollow trees are in short supply, have adapted their hive building techniques to utilize any suitable cavity. This includes spaces inside brick or concrete block walls, small service pits or boxes for either electricity, water or telephone services. Then there are those with more bizarre or macabre tastes in housing, choosing square steel house posts, disused garden incinerators, tyres on old wheels and even hollow tombstones for their residential address. Few of these alternatives offer all the facilities provided by the hollow tree, but nevertheless colonies have been known to survive and even thrive in some of these locations.

Hollow trees not only offer protection from wind and rain, but usually also provide good insulation against temperature extremes. This is important: our stingless bees are not as efficient at maintaining a constant hive temperature as their introduced rival, the honey bee. It is this aspect, together with the fact that they won't (or can't) fly off on foraging missions until the thermometer reaches about 18 degrees centigrade that limits the range of our stingless bees mainly to the tropical, sub-tropical and warmer temperate areas of Australia.

A stingless bees' nest in an old log can make an attractive garden feature. (Photo courtesy Bob Luttrell).

Darryl Bitossi with another example of his unique and unusual hive designs.

So for some stingless bee enthusiasts the easiest way to keep them is to cut out the section of log housing the nest, bring it home and then set it up in a corner of the garden. It may be necessary to raise it off the ground a bit to deter ants, or to put an old stump cap or something similar on top of the log to prevent the entry of rain, but otherwise it's a pretty simple exercise. Furthermore, an old weathered hardwood log, tastefully positioned, can provide an attractive and durable garden feature.

However, for the real enthusiast with an enquiring mind or a scientific interest, the natural log hive has limitations. Consequently, a variety of artificial hives have been developed that incorporate features such as:

- A two-part hive design that allows propagation through splitting of the component parts;

- A glass or clear plastic observation panel whereby some of the internal hive behaviour can be observed; and

- Separate honey 'supers', which facilitate the extraction of tangy bush honey uncontaminated by pollen and brood material.

There are now many artificial hive designs including those that externally resemble small honey bee hives, or round tubing 'artificial logs', to more whimsical shapes such as quaint miniature cottages.

Given that there has already been some commercialisation of stingless bees for crop pollination and boutique honey production, there is an argument for standardizing the artificial hive design in much the same way that honey bee hives are now uniform. However, there is an opposing point of view suggesting that stingless beehive design is still developing and premature standardisation could preclude the introduction of further improvements. Besides, unlike honey bees that are kept almost exclusively for honey production, our stingless bees are often kept for other reasons including conservation or just for the joy and interest of having them in the garden. Also, as there are as many as twelve different Australian species, a one-size fits all artificial hive design is unlikely to evolve in the near future.

Artificial Hive Designs

Stingless beekeepers are continuing to experiment with different hive shapes, volumes and construction materials, which makes it impossible in a publication of this nature to provide details of the latest developments. A photograph (see page 30), kindly provided by the Australian Native Bee Research Centre (ANBRC), shows a collection of designs in

*Col Webb is another prominent stingless beekeeper from southeast Queensland. Col is shown here with one of his special **Austroplebeia australis** hives during a workshop demonstration. **Austroplebeia** spp. possess two features that make them more suitable than **Trigona** bees for such display hives. Firstly they are less inclined to obscure the transparent panels with cerumen and secondly they usually don't enclose their brood completely within an involucrum thereby making observation of their brood structure easier (as seen on page 11). Please note that stingless bee nests cannot tolerate indefinite exposure to the light. Col will replace the timber box that normally covers the transparent panels immediately after the demonstration.*

use at the time of writing. Most of these are quite innovative and have special features relative to the requirements of particular species of bee or local climatic conditions. If you would like more detailed information about these designs you need to refer to the "Native Bees of Australia Series" booklets produced by the ANBRC (see Contacts and Resources section). These individual booklets have the capacity to be revised at short notice to incorporate any significant new hive designs.

*Villagers in Cuetzalan, Mexico continue with traditional methods of stingless beekeeping, preferring to house their **Scaptotrigona mexicana** bees in terracotta pot hives. The inside of one of these hives can be seen on page 9. (Photo courtesy Prof Carlos Vergara)*

Leaving aside the appealing miniature cottages and their ilk, we will now turn to some practical stingless beehive designs. These can currently be divided into two basic concepts – the square (or rectangular) box hive and the round tubular hive. We'll deal with them through representative samples of each type.

The details of the hives shown are as follows (top row, left to right): 1. John Klumpp's design (unpainted); 2. Denis Shepherd's design; 3. Bill Milne's design featuring an outer box enclosing an inner box for extra insulation; 4. Tom Carter's design with the entrance in the top box; 5. Russell Zabel's design including tropical lid. Bottom row: 6. Tim Heard's OATH design; 7. Peter Davenport's design with a painted foam cover; 8. Robert Raymond's design with a metal lid; 9. Les Felhaber's horizontal design with a foam cover (Photos courtesy Dr Anne Dollin)

Square or Rectangular Hives

The OATH

At its most basic the Original Australian Trigona Hive is a rectangular box which is made in two separate halves so that it can be divided horizontally at the midpoint. It is constructed entirely of 25mm (one inch) dressed pine boards and its external dimensions are 28 cm long x 20 cm wide by 24.5 cm high. These dimensions give an internal hive volume of approximately 7 litres.

The boards that form the top and bottom of the hive may be cut to a length of 30 cm to provide a 2 cm overhang at the top and a similar extension at floor level, the latter serving as a landing board. A 12 mm entrance hole is provided in the bottom box a little above this landing board. The OATH is usually painted white on the outside to assist in reflecting summer heat.

As its name indicates this hive was initially intended to house Trigona bees. Although Dr Tim Heard invented it in the early days of keeping stingless bees in artificial hives, it has stood the test of time and remains the basis for most of the designs in use today.

The standard OATH

The Modified OATHs

Modifying an OATH sounds like something a politician might do to a campaign promise after being elected, but I am referring to the changes that some stingless beekeepers have made to the Original Australian Trigona Hive design over time.

Stingless beekeepers are an innovative lot, and there are many successful variations on the original OATH theme out there. I trust those innovators will forgive me if I confine my description here to just one design, which incorporates a number of the more significant modifications.

While retaining the same external dimensions as the OATH, Russell Zabel has incorporated a number of distinctive features into his hive design. Not only can Russell's hives be split at the midpoint, they also include a removable lid which allows for easier inspection, especially when an observation panel in the form of a piece of clear plastic or glass is installed under this cover. Another board is fixed above the lid on 25mm thick spacers. The air gap between the two creates a 'tropical roof' effect.

Initially constructed throughout with 25mm Cypress Pine boards, Russell later increased the thickness of the walls to 45mm to provide better insulation although this has considerably reduced the internal volume of the hive. A special fitting, made from PVC tubing, is attached to one side of the hive so that it can be easily mounted on a standard 'Y' bar ('star') picket.

Russell Zabel's Modified OATH design.

Round Hives

The KITH

Several years ago I set myself the challenge of trying to make a hive that duplicates, as far as practicable, the bees' natural nesting sites within hollow trees. After many trips back to the drawing board I came up with a round plastic tubing design. Not wishing to take the design or myself too seriously I named it the KITH, an acronym for Klumppy's Insulated Tubing Hive.

These insulated tubing hives (KITHs) are displayed in both complete and dismantled form to show the component parts.

This design will never be a universal favourite. The high cost of the materials used, plus the need for special jigs and tight tolerances, means these hives are not only more expensive but also more difficult to make in the home workshop than timber designs. That aside, I have listed below a number of desirable features that inspired the KITH and which hive building readers might like to consider including in their own designs, especially if they are trying to keep our stingless bees in marginal climatic areas or outside their natural range altogether.

Durability and low maintenance: – The main components of the hive, namely the internal and external plastic tubes, are commercial building products that have been designed to withstand the elements - reputedly for in excess of 75 years. Shorter life components are protected from the weather by the hive design. For example, the external plywood bottom board has been recessed into the base of the hive. Should these latter mentioned components eventually deteriorate the design allows them to be easily replaced without disturbing the bees.

The need for special jigs and tight tolerances makes KITHs more difficult to produce in the home workshop.

Insulation against heat and cold: – The original motivation for designing this hive was to try to duplicate the insulating properties of a hollow tree trunk. A thick layer of foam between the hive walls, combined with foam discs within the base and under the roof, encapsulates the bees' living space within insulating material.

To further assist with cooling, four tubes extend vertically through the insulated walls, aligning with holes in the bottom board and in the foam disc below the roof. An air gap is also provided under the roof. This construction allows air to flow around the nest compartment.

During the winter months the bottom board and upper foam disc can be rotated one quarter of a turn to close off the air circulation. For colder climates, a heater is being designed to fit to the base of the hive to allow warm air to flow through the tubes and up to the roof to envelop the hive in warmth.

Two-part design allows propagation by the splitting method: – The KITH can be separated at the midline into two halves and reassembled with the corresponding parts of a new empty hive to enable propagation of a colony by the 'splitting' method.

The hive parts are held together by the centre strapping, which is secured by 6 small screws. This provides for a firm attachment and alignment of the halves. This arrangement also reduces the chance of pests such as ants, phorid flies and syrphid flies getting into a nest when it is most vulnerable just after the split. The galvanized strapping also provides the method whereby the hive can be secured to a steel post or tree etc.

The roof of the KITH is fixed to the rest of the hive with 3 special fastenings, but a short anti clockwise twist is all that is required to remove it to expose the black insulating disk and beneath that the transparent observation panel.

Easy access and inspection facility: – Not only does this feature help you to monitor the progress of a hive after splitting or transfer, it also enhances the enjoyment of keeping the bees by enabling you to observe at least some of the inner workings of the hive. An inspection can be done with minimal disturbance to the bees through the glass observation panel.

The roof of the KITH is firmly affixed to the hive with three special locking lugs, but additional security, such as a small padlock, can be easily installed. The roof is simply removed by a short anti-clockwise twist that exposes a black foam disk lying in a deep recess at the top of the hive. Lifting out this disk (which serves the dual purpose of insulation and excluding light from the hive) reveals the clear observation panel and the hive's interior.

A word of caution here: try not to expose the inside of the nest to full sunlight. Doing so will not only alarm the workers, but prolonged exposure may also damage any visible brood cells. Night inspections with torchlight are safer and more rewarding without the daytime reflections on the glass to contend with.

Anti-slump protection: – In areas that experience high temperatures, stingless beekeepers know only too well how excessive heat can soften the bees' cerumen building material. In some cases this can result in the whole internal structure of the hive collapsing, killing bees, brood and sometimes the whole nest.

Features of the KITH design help to reduce the likelihood of such a disaster. The internal walls of the hive are lined with fine mesh gutter-guard to provide firm anchor points for the bees' construction. Also the round hive shape itself, being more like a tree hollow, eliminates the longer diagonals of a square or rectangular design and, by corresponding more naturally with the shape of the brood structure at the heart of the hive, leaves less of the heavy honey pots unsupported.

Entrances: – An entrance tube is provided in each half, but on opposite sides of the hive. Both slope downward to prevent the entry of rain and are roughened internally to aid the bees' progress in and out. The front entrance in the lower half can be fitted with a landing board if required, but experience has shown this is not necessary. The rear entrance in the upper half is usually blocked off unless required. This entrance (on an empty hive) can be used for 'eduction' or 'budding', which we will discuss later.

Matching Accessories

Keeping stingless bees in artificial hives might provide us with better opportunities to observe, manage and propagate our little charges, but there are always issues to address with the keeping of any creature. Stingless beekeepers have responded with a number of unique devices, hive attachments and accessories. Representative examples have been included in the following categories.

Hive placement & security

In section 9 we will deal with installing and moving hives but here we need to consider the devices necessary to safely and securely fix our artificial hives in place and to ensure that the bees within suffer minimal disturbance. The heavy old log hive that was such a struggle for you to get into your backyard is hardly likely to be blown down in a storm or knocked over by domestic pets or the visiting grand children during their football match, but an artificial hive may be a different story. Unlike some of the round designs, OATHs have a relatively large base area and a low profile which makes them stable enough to position on a flat surface or a purpose built stand, such as those used by honey bee keepers in Queensland to keep their bees out of the reach of cane toads. Even so, as we have already seen, Russell Zabel has decided to use a special fitting made from PVC tubing to mount his modified OATHs on steel pickets. These socalled 'star' pickets are popular with a number of stingless beekeepers. They are inexpensive, easy to drive into the ground,

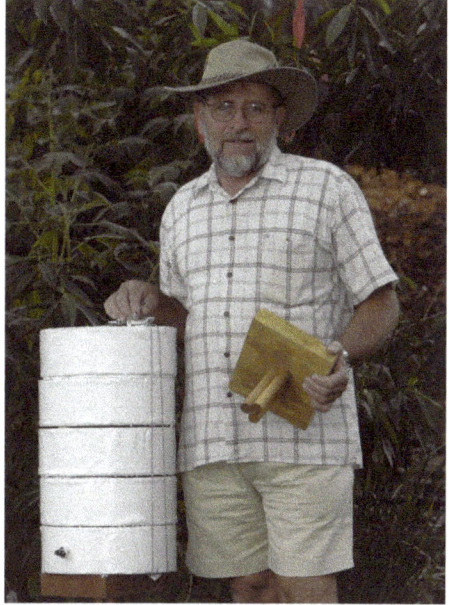

Bob Luttrell is also experimenting with a heavily insulated round hive design and is subjecting his prototypes to rigorous temperature testing. Here he is shown holding the flat base he designed to fit on top of a star picket to support the hive, which is firmly secured to this base with heavy wire strapping. (Photo courtesy Bob Luttrell)

This special bracket fashioned from a short length of star picket allows the KITH to be fixed directly to a tree, or with the addition of a galvanised hook, suspended from a beam, wall or fence

provide a reasonably stable platform for the hive, are easily ant-proofed and if the hive is firmly bolted to the holes in the picket, they provide some deterrent to the casual thief. The galvanised version, which costs only a couple of dollars more than the common black picket, is not only cleaner to handle and more attractive but also very durable in the ground.

A padlock fitted to a hive may provide extra security for your hive.

The versatility of star pickets does not end there. Cut into short sections they can easily be fashioned into tree or wall brackets by the average handy person as shown in the accompanying photographs. This increases the placement options and may enable you to position your hive out of harms way.

Security may be an issue in some situations. A small additional fitting allows the roof of the KITH to be secured with a padlock. This can be particularly useful in display situations or in schools, to prevent constant opening by curious visitors or children.

Climate control and ventilation

Despite our best intentions it is difficult to duplicate in our artificial hives the conditions available to the bees in ideal natural locations. For example can we ever design a small wooden box or foam and plastic tube to match the insulating properties inside a large standing hollow tree during a summer heatwave, where the bees' nest might not only be surrounded by very thick timber, but also benefit from the cooling effects of the air column within the tree? The answer is we can try and with the aid of some modern materials and technology we may be able to get pretty close. We must also remember that our bees are adaptive little creatures and are not always found in ideal conditions in nature and yet they often survive very well in such situations.

Where hives cannot be placed in areas of reasonable shade during the hotter parts of the day an artificial shade cover can be installed. The circular shade umbrella installed above this KITH can be tipped backwards to allow inspection inside the hive.

Many beekeepers use close fitting polystyrene foam covers to insulate their timber hives against temperature extremes. Darryl Bitossi of Brisbane made this smart looking design.

Basically, climate control consists of providing them with shade and insulation against the summer heat and warmth and insulation against the winter cold. Simple enough, but what do you do when the cool shady spot you chose for your new hive last summer turns out to be a freezing cold location through winter? Insulation can help and simply using thicker materials for hive construction can provide some buffer against the cold or the heat. Home building insulation products may be utilised in some situations and both polyurethane and polystyrene foams are recognised insulating materials. Some hive builders are incorporating these products in their designs, others are using polystyrene foam (usually recovered from discarded fruit and vegetable boxes) to build insulating covers for their timber hives.

As the interest in stingless beekeeping has grown so to has the desire to keep them in marginal climatic conditions or outside their natural range altogether. Technology may be the answer here with some innovative people experimenting with artificial heating systems for hives. There are problems to overcome, but who knows, today we take the widespread keeping of tropical fish in heated aquaria for granted; maybe one day heated hives combined with supplementary feeding can extend the range of stingless beekeeping.

Excessively hot weather can also be a problem and in extreme cases the cerumen structure inside some artificial hives has been known to melt down with disastrous consequences for the bees. Where hives cannot be placed under trees or other areas of suitable shade then shade cloth or some other similar material can be utilised to provide protection from the summer heat. This offers an additional advantage in that it can be removed during the cooler months so the bees can warm up in the winter sunshine.

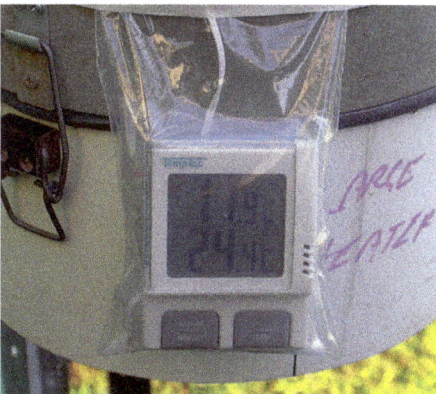

These three photographs show the construction, testing and installation of a prototype heater design for a KITH. Using car light bulbs as a gentle heat source these 12-volt, thermostatically controlled devices are safe out of doors. The heat generated travels through the passageways designed for cooling in summer and envelopes the hive in warmth during the colder months. In this case the heater has raised the core temperature of the hive more than 12 degrees above the ambient temperature of 11.9 degrees. Heaters may be useful for nursing a weak hive through the winter period and for assisting hives being kept in cooler areas that are considered marginal for the keeping of stingless bees. One day such heaters may be used for keeping these bees well south of their natural range.

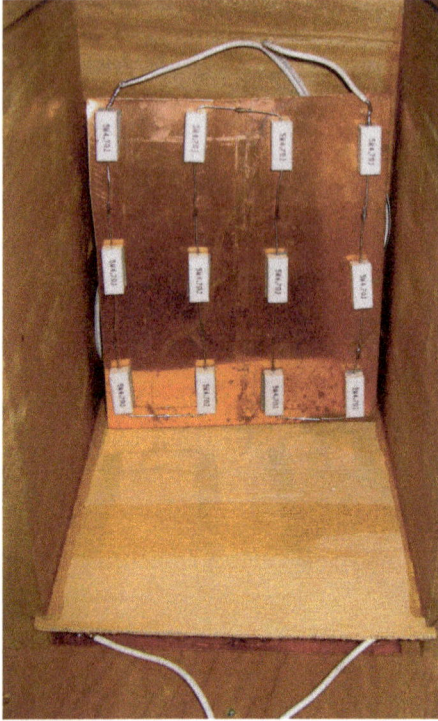

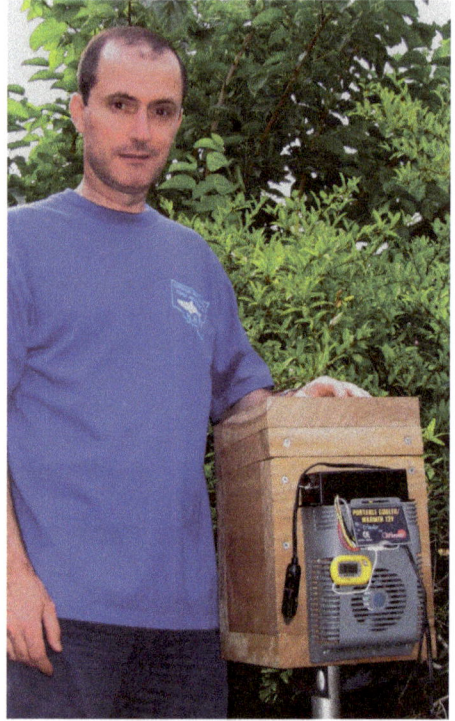

Carlos Alonso, shown in the accompanying photo, is developing an internal underfloor heater system for timber hives. The small electrical resistors mounted on copper plate are at the heart of this unit. They draw little power and may be able to deliver the warmth just where it is needed on frosty winter nights. (Two photos courtesy Carlos Alonso)

Not content to confine his inventiveness to heaters, Carlos has also been experimenting with evaporative and refrigerated cooling systems ever since the Sydney heatwave in 2006 when many stingless bee colonies in artificial hives were lost. This prototype uses a small commercially available refrigerated cooling unit to reduce the temperature in a hive.

Ventilation is another important issue that we sometimes tend to overlook. In natural situations colonies enclose themselves within walls of hard cerumen (often mixed with other materials) that is known as the batumen. However, this layer is not as solid or impervious as it may first appear. Usually the bees will incorporate a number of small holes in the batumen structure, not only to allow the intake of fresh air, but equally importantly to vent carbon dioxide and the excess moisture produced through the evaporative technique employed to convert nectar to honey.

In artificial hives (particularly those housing colonies that are strong and well developed) the bees may keep open drain holes in the floor, tiny cracks in the hive joints or spaces beneath observation panels and the like as substitutes for the purpose built vents they would maintain in a natural batumen. I include a back entrance in all my KITHs and rather than sealing it up completely when not required I now use a special ventilated plug which the bees modify over time with the addition or removal of cerumen to maintain the level of ventilation they require. These same plugs are also used in the main entrance whenever I need to transfer a hive to another location. The bees cannot escape, but they have adequate ventilation which is especially important during hot weather. An alternative solution is to seal them in with a small twist of shade cloth, or tape fine mesh over the entrance, but a purpose built ventilated plug is both easier and more effective.

*The batumen is a layer of hard cerumen mixed with other materials that encloses and protects a stingless bee colony in a natural location such as a tree hollow. Here a section of batumen from a rescued **Trigona carbonaria** nest is held up to the light to reveal the pattern of tiny holes used to provide ventilation*

These ventilated entrance plugs were designed for KITHs, but will fit any hive with a suitable entrance diameter. Very handy when moving hives they have been made by utilizing a small soldering iron to weld fly screen mesh to the end of a short piece of black plastic tubing.

Artificial feeders

While there is some difference of opinion on the subject, a significant number of beekeepers believe that, in certain circumstances, artificial feeding is of benefit to their stingless bees. They are convinced it can assist in getting a weak hive on its feet or carry it through rough times when there are few plants in flower.

When transferring a nest from a log into an artificial hive it is not desirable to install broken or damaged honey pots in the bees' new home. Consequently such hives may be placed in a starvation situation, especially if bad weather follows the transfer and prevents them foraging. However, with care, the honey can be recovered from the damaged honey pots by squeezing them and straining the contents through a fine mesh. This can be gradually fed back to the bees, but keep the excess in the freezer. Stingless bee honey has a higher moisture content than honey bee honey and this factor combined with some impurities such as pollen grains may cause it to ferment if it is not kept cold.

However, more often than not, stingless beekeepers will use a sugar and water mix or diluted honey bee honey for feeding purposes. For those like me who favour the latter option opinions vary on the rate of dilution with water. I use a ratio of 75% honey to 25% water by volume and find this is well accepted by my bees.

Artificial feeder designs range from simply piercing a single serve honey sachet with a fine point and suspending it near the hive entrance to complicated devices that deliver the mixture inside the hive itself. One thing you cannot do is simply place an open container of honey in or near the hive. The bees will lose their footing and drown in what is an ocean of food to them. So feeders have been designed to supply the food at a controlled rate, either by capillary action as in a sponge, by seeping slowly from a small vent or by the method I prefer, from around the edges of a descending float.

Bill Milne originally came up with the idea of using the descending float arrangement to feed his stingless bees. I have simply modified his design over time and now produce two slightly different models based on his original concept. I found that discarded black 35mm film canisters held a suitable amount of liquid food, prevented the entry of rain when the lid is pressed back in place, were durable in the weather and excluded sunlight which might adversely affect the contents. The internal floating disk, which is simply dropped on top of the honey and water mixture after the canister has been filled to an appropriate level, is cut from thin nylon cutting board with a hole-saw. It floats low enough to allow the bees easy access to the honey and water mix from around the edges or from small holes drilled through the disk.

The accompanying photographs, which show the two versions of the feeder in cutaway section, make detailed description unnecessary. The Mark 1 feeder has a row of 3mm holes near the top to allow stingless bees access (but not honey bees) and is slipped into a wire frame positioned near the hive entrance.

The Mark 2 feeder evolved later and has a single larger hole, which enables it to be plugged onto a modified plastic 'Tee' piece that has been inserted into the hive's entrance. This design is more secure in terms of excluding honey bees and other insects because the guard bees take up position at the front of their new entrance extension. It also allows the stingless bees to access the food mix during bad weather. As a result this feeder functions much like one positioned inside the hive, yet it is far easier to access for cleaning and refilling. However, it is restricted to use on artificial hives with a suitable entrance diameter, whereas the earlier model can be attached to any hive type including natural logs.

Mark 1 feeder shown in cutaway section.

Mark 2 feeder shown in cutaway section.

The component parts used in construction of the descending float feeders. Disks are cut from nylon cutting board and the entrance extension is fashioned from a 'Tee' shaped plastic garden irrigation fitting.

A full Mark 2 feeder installed on hive. Note the cordon of guard bees stationed at the extended entrance.

Honey Supers

Dr Tim Heard not only invented the Original Australian Trigona Hive, which initiated stingless beekeeping in artificial hives, he is also at the forefront in developing techniques to produce stingless bee honey. At the time of writing Tim was working with the Australian Native Bee Research Centre to produce a specific publication on harvesting honey from stingless bees. Please refer to the Contacts section for details on how to obtain ANBRC publications.

*Tim Heard's honey super design for **Trigona** bees. The super is designed to make honey harvesting more effective by keeping the honeypots separate from the brood and pollen storage areas of the hive. (Photo courtesy Tim Heard)*

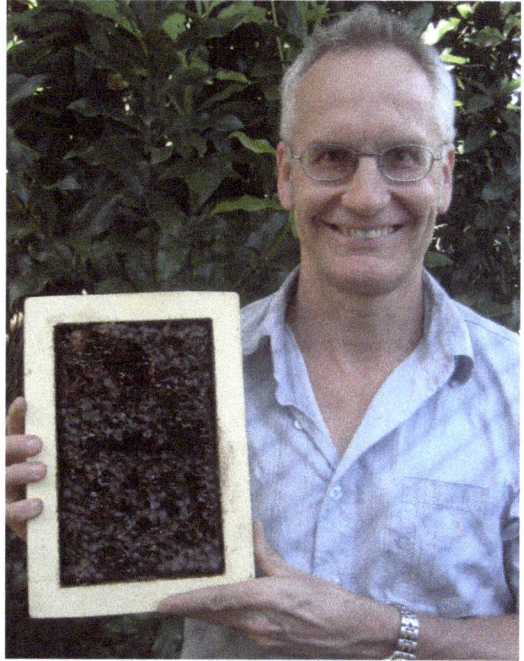

*Dr. Tim Heard is pictured here holding one of his honey supers packed with **Trigona carbonaria** honey pots full of tangy bush honey. (Photo courtesy Tim Heard)*

These two photos show the super full of the hive's honey treasure. Tim uses a multi-pronged tool to pierce the honey pots before allowing their contents to drain into a clean container. After straining through a fine mesh the tangy sugarbag honey is ready for consumption. (Photos courtesy Tim Heard)

Hive Propagation Accessories

Most accessories associated with reproducing hives are inextricably linked with the techniques involved in propagation and have therefore been included in those specific sections.

However, there are a couple of exceptions and the most notable of these is Col Webb's innovative floor board. When a hive is split the usual practice is for the old bottom half to receive a new top while the old top part (without an entrance) is placed on an empty bottom half. This second situation can be unstable and may result in the contents of the top box collapsing unless properly supported at the midpoint of the two halves.

Col has removed this concern with the design of his special floor board, which incorporates an entrance, supporting wire mesh and drain holes. The full top half of the old hive is placed directly on this floor board rather than on top of an empty half box, which eliminates any chance of it slumping. The honey leaking from the honey pots broken as a result of the split can drain away and this half of the hive is now furnished with its own entrance, built into the floor board. This means both parts of the split are provided with new empty top halves, enabling both colonies to expand upwards.

Col also utilises what he refers to as his 'bee tent' to temporarily house hives that have been recently rescued or split. Another stingless beekeeper, Alan Stewart, has designed a more permanent structure for this purpose. The aim is to provide protection against the elements as well as against pests and invaders until the bees have completed their repairs and order is restored in the colonies.

Col Webb's innovative floor board design incorporates an entrance, supporting wire mesh and drain holes in the one unit.

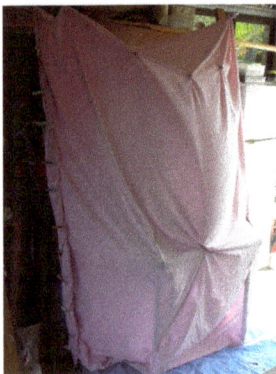

Col Webb and Alan Stewart have each developed methods for protecting newly split hives. Col's bee tent appears on the left and Alan's more elaborate structure is on the right.

8. Buying a Hive

(Illustration by Phillipa van Gilst)

For many people, the most convenient (and economical) way of obtaining their own stingless bee colony is to buy an established hive. Sometimes colonies in logs are offered for sale, but for reasons mentioned earlier most people with a keen interest in stingless bees will want to acquire an artificial hive sooner or later. Besides, purchasing colonies in logs could encourage unscrupulous sellers to harvest too many nests from our natural bushland. Insisting on an artificial hive with a replacement warranty not only discourages this practice, but also offers you greater protection.

However, such conditions come at a cost, and a premium product usually comes with a higher price tag. As with so many things you get what you pay for, but a little bit of knowledge gained beforehand will make you a more discerning buyer and may help to avoid disappointment down the track.

Firstly, the material that the hive is made out of is important, even more important than that used for honey bee hives. This is because honey bees construct (or re-use) vertical combs suspended within the hive on removable wooden frames for storing honey, pollen and their brood. If the outer box rots away over time, it's an inconvenience for a beekeeper, but he or she can simply transfer the frames containing the combs into a new standard size box (or 'Super' as the ones above the brood are known) and, hey presto, the hive has a new home. To stingless bees the box itself is the foundation of their construction. Overlapping pollen and honey pots are attached directly to the floor, walls and ceiling. A box that rots away quickly in the weather is going to be a major problem for native bees and their keeper. Also, honey bees have a prodigious capacity for warming and cooling their hive so the insulating properties of the box material are not as important as they are for our stingless bees which cannot maintain a constant temperature as effectively as the introduced bee.

A strong Trigona carbonaria colony inside an OATH. Note how they have firmly attached all their structure to the inside of the hive. (Photo courtesy Lyndall Rosevear)

So what should the stingless beekeeper use? Well, it would make things less expensive all round if we could build hives out of cheap old chipboard (known as 'Weet-Bix' in the trade, because it swells and falls apart in flakes when it gets damp) but that is not a real option even for hives kept under cover because the bees themselves generate moisture when they evaporate the nectar to produce honey. I know there are some water resistant composite boards on the market, but I would be wary of them, not only because the chemicals used in their manufacture might adversely affect the bees, but the absorption of those chemicals into the honey might also adversely affect any of us humans who decide to drizzle it on our ice-cream. This leaves us with exterior ply (or better yet Marine bondwood) or solid timber to construct our hives.

Now I'm no expert on timber, but my father was a carpenter so I picked up a little bit of knowledge over the years. It stands to reason that the thicker the timber the better its insulating properties and, for a given thickness, the pines are better insulators than the heavier hardwoods. For this reason, most hives are constructed from pine despite the better durability of hardwood. Various wall thicknesses are used, and some beekeepers build close fitting covers cut from polystyrene foam to improve insulation, but this does tend to retain moisture around the timber and may add to the problem of rotting. The quick growing plantation pines, such as Radiata, produce suitably- sized boards (albeit full of knots) that are usually cheaply priced in the larger hardware stores. Unfortunately this timber is not durable out of doors. It is fine for your cupboard shelving, but in my opinion is unsuitable for constructing stingless beehives. Chemically treated pine boards, while durable, are of course not suitable due to their toxicity. Overseas timbers, especially those that have come into Australia in the form of packing crates should also be treated with caution, not only in terms of their durability, but also because they may have been fumigated or subjected to other treatments that may be toxic to the bees (and people alike).

Good hives are constructed from durable quality timbers. They will be painted on the outside, so you may have to ask the seller about the type of wood that has been used in the construction.

Some innovative stingless beekeepers have not confined themselves to timber for their hive construction. I've seen hives built from materials including terracotta, concrete and a concrete and clay mix. The latter mentioned may be durable, but my back isn't up to moving the larger ones around and they tend to stay damp and cold in winter.

I've gone off in a different direction altogether, as discussed earlier, and make mine from plastic tubing. One drawback is the cost of this tubing in the large diameter sizes required. When I first started building these hives, I spent much of my time scrounging around large building sites plying plumbers and drainers with expensive bottles of alcohol in exchange for their off-cuts.

Regardless of the material used to build the hive be sure to carefully check out the quality of construction. A well-made hive should have neat, close fitting components to help keep out pests and invaders. All joints should be well-secured and the hive properly painted to maximise its life in all weathers. Provision should be made on the hive for it to be securely mounted up off the ground on a post, tree or wall where it can be better protected against ant attack and dampness. Ideally, your artificial hive should also have a transparent observation panel under the roof. This will allow you to watch some of the internal workings of the colony inside without causing much disturbance.

*While a hive being offered for sale may not be brim-full with structure, it should nevertheless contain a reasonable amount of brood and a good population of bees as shown in this **Trigona carbonaria** hive. It is interesting to note, in this photograph, that the new brood cells, which are darker in colour, are advancing strongly upwards just below the remnants of the paler mature cells hatching out above.*

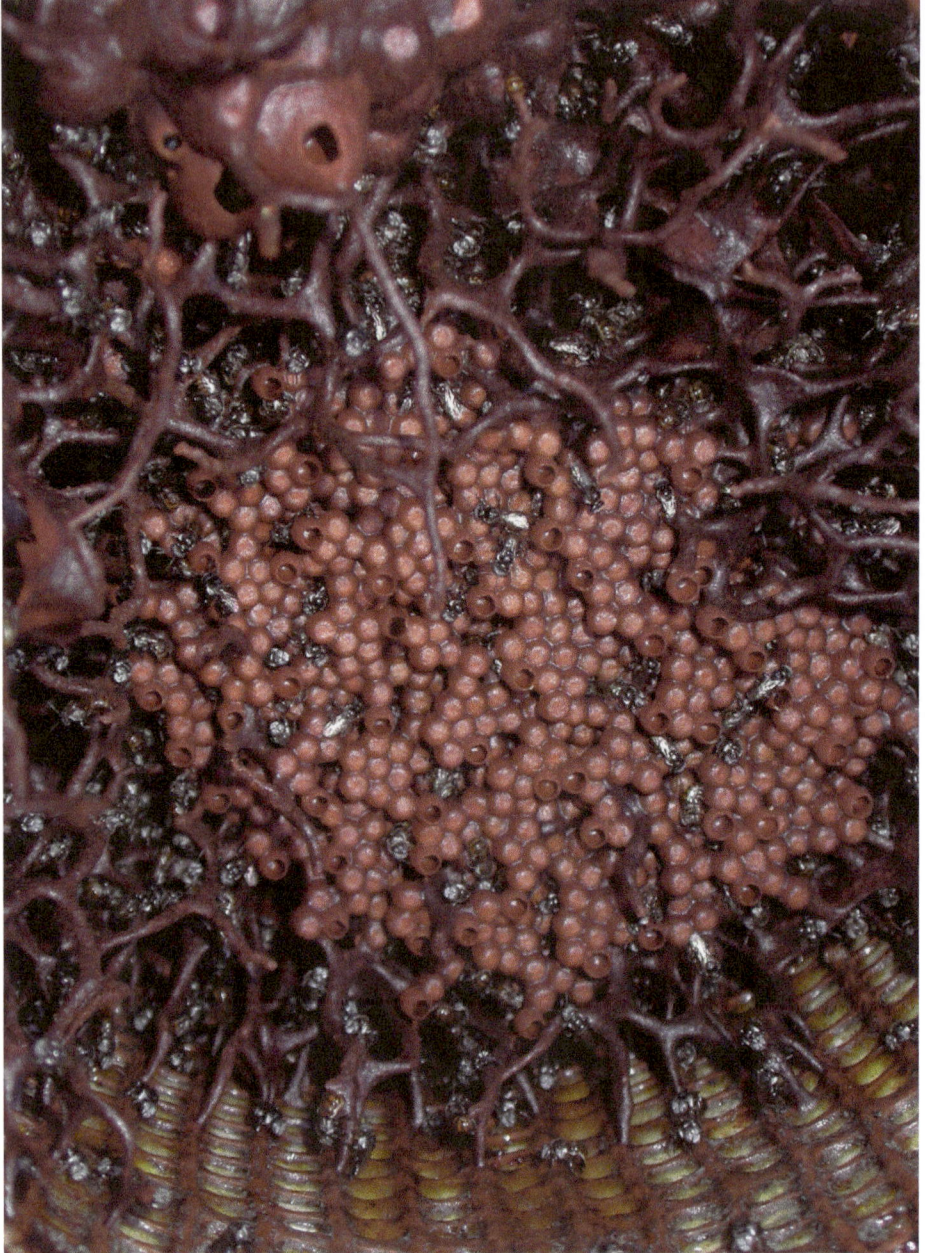

*This young **Trigona hockingsi** nest contains clean, firm structure without any sign of pests or invaders, a healthy brood comb and an appropriate number of bees for its size. In time it should develop into a strong hive.*

Now that we've dealt with the packaging, what about the most important bit of all – the bees themselves.

Most reputable dealers will allow you to inspect a hive before you buy. Arrange to drop around on a warm and sunny day between 10 am to 3pm.

*The resin and other deposits around this **Trigona carbonaria** entrance suggest it is a well-established hive. The entrances of other species will not accumulate this amount of deposited resin.*

Check out the hive entrance – is it dirty looking and smeared with sticky resin? Dirty is good in this case. It suggests the hive (or at least the part containing the entrance) has been established for some time.

Look to see how much bee 'traffic' there is at the entrance, the more the better. Now check a bit closer to see what that traffic is doing. Are some bees returning with bundles of pollen in their pollen baskets? This is a good sign. Pollen is the protein food of the hive and is used for feeding the larvae. Is the occasional bee leaving the entrance with a little brown 'package'? If so, this is even better. These little packages are the old pupae cases that are discarded as new bees hatch out of the brood. Occasionally a dead bee will also be hauled out and discarded. This is quite normal. They don't hold much of a funeral service in a stingless bee colony - losses are occurring all the time, but a good queen will be producing enough eggs to maintain the hive's strength.

Depending on the circumstances the seller may offer to let you inspect the inside of the hive. If the hive is fitted with an observation panel you should insist on taking a look. Don't expect to find a hive full to the very brim. Even the most reputable seller is unlikely to offer for sale a hive ready for splitting, but the hive should contain a reasonable amount of structure, and most importantly there should be a good number of bees. Honey and pollen pots should be visible on the walls and the brood (or the involucrum housing the brood) should form a significant proportion of the hive.

*The powdery appearance inside this **Austroplebeia australis** hive has been caused by mites destroying the pollen pots and dispersing the pollen. (Photo courtesy Lee Byrnes)*

If, in addition to the bees, you spot a number of small insects that look like overweight humpbacked vinegar flies darting quickly about inside the hive and/or a number of white 'maggots' on the pollen or honey pots don't buy it. These are phorid fly and their larvae. They are a major pest for stingless bees and can wipe out a hive. Similarly, if there is loose powdery pollen inside the hive, give it a miss. This is caused by pollen pots being destroyed, their contents dispersed by pollen mites, and is also not a good sign.

Other indications of a good hive include the weight of the contents. At least one kilogram, preferably two, helps to indicate a healthy hive. Smelling the hive also gives you an idea of its well-being. It should have a pleasant aromatic "nose". A sour smell can indicate that there is an infestation of syrphid flies.

If everything inside the hive looks satisfactory, ask the seller if he or she offers any guarantee on the hive's survival. Most reputable sellers will give a conditional guarantee on a hive for up to 12 months; agreeing to replace the hive if it should die out in that time.

However, a seller can't be expected to replace a hive if it is lost due to mismanagement, or just plain stupidity. Most sellers stipulate a range of circumstances where they won't make reparation which include:

- spraying insecticides in or around the hive (including lawn grub spray);
- dropping or shaking the hive;
- exposing the hive to extremes of heat or cold;
- opening the hive up excessively;
- failing to take adequate precautions to protect the new hive from invasion by ants and other pests; and
- attempting to keep the bees outside their natural climatic range.

Okay, so you've liked everything you've seen during the inspection and after haggling with the seller over the price you figure that provided the kids can go without shoes for another year you can afford it. Despite your enthusiasm, just remember that you won't be able to take it home there and then. Unless you want to lose a lot of foragers you will have to wait until after dark before the hive can be sealed up for transport. If it is inconvenient for you to return in the evening make firm arrangements to pick it up on a subsequent day at a certain time. The seller will close up the hive entrance the night before you are due to call back and will usually put the hive in a cool sheltered area to prevent overheating. Being stingless, our little social bees can also be sent through the mail or carried by a courier service provided the seller is agreeable to such an arrangement.

In the meantime, decide on a suitable place in your garden or on your verandah or patio for your hive. Remember, if you change your mind later on, you can't simply switch it to another corner of the garden, as you will lose a lot of foragers; so choose your spot carefully in the first place. Refer to the section on Installing and Moving Hives, which also gives advice on how to go about relocating a hive in your yard if you really do need to move it at any time.

On the way home with your hive don't stop to do the grocery shopping and leave it in your car in the hot sun. If you must break your journey, put the hive in a cool spot. An airconditioned room or office won't hurt the bees, but the heat inside a closed car in the sun, even on a winter's day, can reach a point where it will soften the bees' cerumen building material and the whole contents of the hive may slump and kill the colony.

9. Installing and Moving Hives

The hive outside my window provides a welcome distraction.

When I first brought home the hive I can see from my window, I positioned it with care. I knew that trying to re-locate it to another spot in the garden some time later could be a bit of a pain. It's located on the eastern side of my house, so it won't have to endure the cold southwesterly winds that we sometimes experience even here in sunny south east Queensland during the winter months. The general view of stingless beekeepers, which I followed, is that a hive benefits from facing somewhere in the quadrant between north and east and so I pointed its entrance just a little to the north of east.

The hive is mounted on a short steel 'star' picket located under the leaves of a large Cycad. There are no small branches or leaves to swish around the front of the hive and disrupt the flight path of the bees. The hive receives partial sun in the early morning and full shade from about 10am onwards. It is located close to a pathway, but the occasional passer-by does not cause any problems for the bees and vice versa.

The hive had previously been at a distant site, and I had waited there until a little after nightfall to ensure I had retrieved as many foragers as possible before sealing up the entrance with a ventilated plug and bringing it home. A twist of gauze material, shade cloth or even a piece of hosiery poked into the entrance will allow some air to pass through if you don't have a purpose built plug. I installed the hive on the picket the same night, but I did not unseal the entrance until first thing the next morning. Opening the entrance in the dark would possibly have resulted in the loss of any bees that emerged.

Although this wasn't a newly rescued or split colony, and it had its defences in order, I didn't take any chances and installed an ant barrier on the star picket below the hive. For this purpose, I buy packets of extra long pipe cleaners from the major department stores, where they are sold as craft items for young children. Wrapping one of these firmly about the picket and soaking it in oil will discourage even the most determined ants for quite a while.

I made it a point not to disturb the hive in any way for several days. I did not even peer through the observation panel at the bees until I felt they were fully settled into their new location. Instead I relied upon observing their activity at the entrance to get an idea of how they were going. It was soon clear that everything was in order. Foragers were out in force, some bringing back pollen, while other workers concentrated on disposing of the old pupae casings in little brown packages.

The little brown packages being carried out in the bees' jaws are the remains of the cocoons which encased the pupating bees. Unlike the cerumen cells they cannot be recycled and are constantly being discarded.

Trigona carbonaria worker bees struggle to carry the old pupae cases away from the hive before discarding them. (Photo courtesy Marc Newman)

Now that brings me to a few words of caution. I am sometimes asked whether hives can be installed on open verandas, patios and decks. I can see no problem for the bees with this arrangement provided they are in a sheltered position, protected from the extremes of heat, cold and strong winds. However, if you're having the boss over for a posh Sunday luncheon on the deck and your bees keep dropping their little brown packages into his wife's lemonade or champagne you may have trouble explaining the situation.

Similarly, if your Mother-in-law (who does not share your affection for social insects) arrives or the pizza delivery boy calls, they may become alarmed when confronted by bees swarming from the hive next to your front door. So take a little time to consider the suitability of the spot you have chosen for your new hive before opening their front door and turning them loose on your flowers.

But what if your bees are already in the wrong place. What if they are too close to the barbeque table, and keep depositing their rubbish and even their dear departed colleagues in your spouse's potato salad. What can you do? Well, unless you want to lose a large number of bees, you can't suddenly move your hive to the other corner of the yard. Foragers fix the location of their hive in their little brains with precision. Apparently they do this with reference to nearby landmarks. If you move their hive, even by as little as a few metres, they will become disoriented. They will try to return to the old site and may remain there for days or even longer, until they finally all expire.

You have two options if you want to move your bees to another nearby site. The first is to seal their hive up at night and move it away from their foraging area altogether – preferably more than one kilometre. Leave it there for at least two weeks before moving it back at night to the new location. The second method involves moving the hive in very small steps (of less than a metre) each night. The bees may seem a little confused when they first emerge in the morning but they can re-orient themselves over this short distance. You can combine this lateral move with a small change in height as well if you want to raise or lower the hive. You can also rotate the entrance direction slightly each night, which may be all you need to change their flight path – and restore domestic harmony.

Alan Beil calls this long single box hive containing 3 separate Austroplebeia australis colonies his trifecta hive. It is an experimental design intended to minimise hive building materials and conserve the warmth generated by the colonies during the winter months. Trigona bees would probably not be successful in this arrangement because they are notably more belligerent towards other colonies in close proximity. The 'Trifecta' has been positioned to face outwards from under a pergola in a way that avoids any inconvenience to visitors (or the bees) when the area is used for entertaining

This home made 'Bee Mobile' consists of nothing more than a steel picket mounted firmly on an old motor mower base. It enables a hive to be moved easily in small steps of less than a metre each evening.

10. Bee Rescues & Transfers to Artificial Hives

Before I suggest some methods for rescuing and transferring stingless bee colonies I should mention that felling a tree or even just cutting a nest out of already fallen timber is not for the faint-hearted. The process usually requires the use of a chainsaw, wedges and crowbar, often in less than ideal circumstances, and while you are being attacked by bees that don't realise you are trying to do them a good turn. Safety should be your paramount concern and if you are not confident in the use of the necessary tools you need to enlist the help of someone who is.

Also, you need to consider the bees' welfare in any felling and transfer exercise and plan accordingly. Wet days are not suitable, neither are cold days or late afternoons if the temperature is likely to drop to 18 degrees centigrade or lower. The bees simply can't fly at these lower temperatures, and will be lost. The brood may also become chilled and die. Ideally, transfers from logs to artificial hives should only be done in spring and early summer to give the colony a chance to recover and build up stores before winter. However, with colony rescues you may not have the luxury of being able to pick and choose the best season. The brood is also sensitive to light and heat, and should be shaded from the sun at all times. Be gentle with them. A friend of mine once described the transfer of a colony from a log into an artificial hive as a deeply traumatic event for both him and the bees, but both survived the process.

Cutting into an old dead hollow tree with a chainsaw in summer can be likened to donning one of those rough 'Hairshirts' worn by religious ascetics for mortification and penance. So for readers who don't feel they need the cathartic experience that comes with the accumulation of sawdust and woodchips in one's underwear on a hot day, there are other ways of obtaining a log containing a stingless bees' nest. Firewood cutters and tree loppers often come across stingless bees and can sometimes be converted from apathy to conservation if plied with offers of alcoholic beverages or other appropriate inducements.

So whether you've cut down an old hollow tree in the path of the developer's bulldozer, or swapped a carton of brown ale for a log destined for the woodcutter's block splitter or chipper, you now have to decide what to do with it. You can of course just choose to leave the colony in the log; in which case you will need to cut it to a suitable length, block up the entrance and any other escape routes and bring it home in the back of your ute, trailer or the boot of your car.

Felling a tree of this size is not for the fainthearted. Alan Beil inspecting a dead tree.

Just a little hint before you go any further. Mark the top of the log with timber crayon or chalk so that, when you are struggling to get it out of your vehicle and up the garden path to its final destination at night, at least you will know which end is up. Installing it upside down could be disastrous for the bees inside, particularly for the brood. It may be necessary to nail a stump cap or piece of tin on the top to protect the hive from the weather. Plastic flowerpot saucers of a suitable diameter, if inverted, will sometimes do the job quite nicely and can be more attractive than the sheet metal options; but pick a heavy duty ultraviolet stabilised saucer, as you (and the bees) want it to last. If possible, install the log so that it is raised up off the ground a little to deter ants and termites, and also to reduce decay.

But the focus of this section is on transferring a nest of bees from a natural log into an artificial hive, so let's return to the paddock at the point where the condemned hollow tree has hit the ground and is surrounded by angry bees. Now, we know they're stingless, but they're not biteless. They can deliver a little nip with their jaws and often target the most sensitive parts of our bodies. Dozens of angry bees applying little pinprick bites to the soft skin around your eyes, nose, ears and armpits can certainly distract you from what you are doing. I've seen big brawny 'bushies' driven from the scene of action by 4mm long Trigona bees acting in concert. The message here is wear the right gear, which includes a midge veil over a wide brimmed hat. Long trousers tucked into the top of your socks and a long-sleeved shirt buttoned at the wrist will complete your bee rescue attire. You may not feature on the cover of a fashion magazine, but you'll feel a lot more comfortable and do a better job of the transfer if you are well protected.

If you've obtained a section of log containing a colony of bees from a firewood cutter, you can probably skip this next bit. However, if you are rescuing a nest from a fallen tree, you will need to get some idea of where to cut above and below the nest entrance so that you are left with a manageable length of log to deal with. In the past I've experimented with drilling holes into the log to try to determine the size of the nest inside the cavity but, in the end, I resorted to the simpler (but noisier) 'hairshirt' alternative. Use your chainsaw

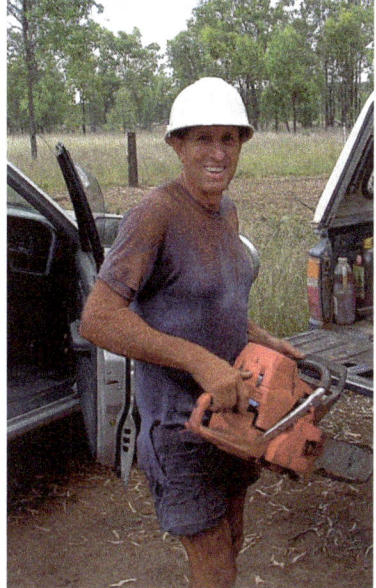

The hairshirt experience. Respected stingless beekeeper and experienced bushman Alan Beil is covered in sawdust after rescuing a bee colony from a dead tree in the path of the new fence line shown in the background. Alan's safety glasses and ear protection have been removed for the photograph, but those who know him will understand that nothing would induce him to remove his iconic white hard hat.

This rescued hive is well protected against rain. It has also been positioned up off the ground away from dampness and to deter ants.

While Lee Byrnes is fairly well protected in his bee rescue attire some stingless bees can be seen trying to gain entry under the short sleeves of his shirt.

to cut through the log well above and well below the entrance. Usually a metre below and the same (or a little less) above the entrance will provide plenty of clearance, but have some regard to the likely diameter of the cavity inside the log. Skinny hollows naturally mean that the bees have to spread their nest further along the cavity to get sufficient living space.

When that's done, roll the log clear of the main tree, utilizing the crowbar and the strong mate you brought along for an outing. Clear out the dirt and debris from the hollow ends of the log, but watch out for the ants, scorpions, spiders, centipedes and any other bitey critters that also called this tree home. Progressively cut slices off the top and bottom of the log and repeat this process until you can feel and see the batumen layers that signify the top and bottom of the hive. Alternatively you can, carefully, use a stick to gauge the start of the nest and then transfer the measurement to the outside of the log before beginning your cut.

By now the bees will be even more stirred up, so let them settle down a bit while you get your equipment ready for the next step in the operation. Open up the top of the artificial hive you brought along so that it is ready to receive the brood. I recommend bringing along an extra hive in case the colony is larger than expected. It may be possible to split the nest into two hives in such circumstances. These hives should be equipped with drain holes or some other feature to allow any honey from broken honey pots to drain away. Have a bucket with a lid ready to receive the excess honey and pollen from the hive.

If you are really handy with the chainsaw and if the nest's entrance is on a knob, lump or bulge (as is often the case) then cut it off neatly and fix it to the front of your hive with 'Blu Tac' or some other non toxic putty-like substance. Failing that remove some of the resinous material from around the old entrance with a pen knife, soften it in your hands and stick it around the entrance of your hive. Some species don't deposit resin around the entrance, so in that case you may need to utilize some cerumen from inside after the log is opened.

Now take a good look at the ends of the log and assess how difficult it would be to split the log lengthways with steel wedges. Some logs that have a straight grain in the timber, and the presence of radial cracks, will split apart very easily. Others can be as hard as the 'hobs of hell', and require repeated thumping with a very large hammer to make any impression at all. This jarring doesn't do the bees any good so, in that case, you are better off using the chainsaw to run longitudinal cuts down opposite sides of the log, increasing the depth with each pass until the log can be prised apart with a crowbar, tyre lever or pinch bar. Before you complete this action get your assistant to unfurl the beach umbrella or tarpaulin you made him carry into the site, and erect it so that your area of operation is in shade. If he forgot this item, at the very least make him hold his broad brimmed hat in a position that protects the brood from the sun.

You will now be faced with a sight of some destruction and confusion, so be prepared to act quickly but gently. The bees' brown cerumen building material will dominate the scene inside

When rescuing or transferring hives it is important to be well prepared, which means having all the necessary gear on hand. (Photo courtesy Bob Luttrell)

*Making longitudinal cuts with the chainsaw is often necessary. Here Alan Beil carefully makes the cut with the chainsaw while Peter Scott is ready to help as soon the **Austroplebeia australis** nest is revealed.*

the opened log. Some honey and pollen pots made of this material will have broken open. Honey will be leaking from them and some of the nest's yellow and orange coloured pollen stores will have become dislodged. In the midst of this seemingly random pattern of storage pots should be the brood cells. As mentioned before, with *Trigona carbonaria* bees these are

*Alan Beil gently removing **Austroplebeia australis** brood from an opened log.*

arranged in a regular broad spiral, usually enclosed in a protective involucrum made from several layers of wafer thin sheets of cerumen, although part of this may have been torn away during the opening process.

Using a knife, sharpened spoon or spatula, collect some of the undamaged honey and pollen pots and carefully arrange them in the bottom of your hive, leaving room in the middle for the brood. Don't try to collect too much in the way of stores, just enough to tide them over until the foragers get going properly again.

Utilize the same implements to gently remove the brood itself together with as much of the involucrum as you can. Be particularly careful with any larger cells you notice on the outer edge of the brood. These are queen cells, and may be vital to the colony's survival if the queen herself has been lost or killed. Also, take note of the way the brood was aligned in the tree and put it into your hive the same way – right side up.

In most cases, it is a waste of time to make an extensive search for the queen. Hopefully she will be hiding away down inside that brood comb you just transferred, but occasionally she will be spotted somewhere else in the remains of the nest. She may try to hide in the myriad cracks and crevices in the old tree hollow. In this event it is very helpful to have a homemade aspirator (or 'Pooter' as the scientists call them – don't ask me why).

You create a vacuum in the collecting chamber (an empty peanut paste jar in this case) by sucking on the shorter plastic tube while directing the other towards the queen bee. This draws her safely into the bottle, her fall cushioned by a thin layer of foam plastic on the bottom. If you decide to make yourself a Pooter, just ensure the bottom end of the suction tube is securely covered by fine mesh gauze as shown or you could find out that queen bees have a slightly nutty flavour but are rather squishy on the palate.

Okay, so you've got the brood safely into your new box along with some provisions, but the success of your transfer is going to depend upon how many bees you can now recover. The old entrance you stuck on the front will help in attracting the bees to their new front door but, in all the confusion caused by the destruction of their old home, they will need a little more help than that. Put the lid back on your artificial hive and try to position it as closely as possible to the spot that was occupied by the old nest prior to the transfer. This may be impossible if the nest was high up in the tree you have just felled. At least try to position it so that it is oriented the same way. You did note which way the old entrance faced before you fired up the chainsaw, didn't you?

Mounting the new hive temporarily on a steel picket driven into the ground at the site of the old nest is recommended. It will hold the hive securely, and keep it up off the ground. A couple of those long pipe cleaners, mentioned previously, soaked in oil, may be needed as ant deterrents. Taping up

Here the rescuer is carefully transferring **Austroplebiea australis** *brood from the opened log into an artificial hive. Chances are the queen will be hiding within this brood mass.(Photo courtesy Bob Luttrell)*

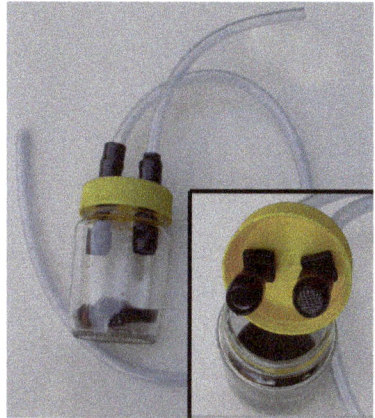

A home-made aspirator or 'pooter', showing the basic components of the device (inset)

Austroplebeia australis *bees entering their new residence which has been positioned as near as possible to the site of their old log home.*

the joints in the hive can also help to prevent attack by other opportunists such as syrphid and phorid flies that are drawn to the scent of a disrupted hive. Given half a chance, they will lay their eggs near cracks and joints so their larvae can later sneak inside. If they gain entry in sufficient numbers, these larvae will destroy the new hive's stores and, ultimately, the colony itself.

It's now time to start cleaning up the remains of the old hive, and in so doing trying to encourage as many bees as possible to look for their new home. Collect the excess of the honey and pollen pots and store them in your clean plastic bucket with a lid. Blow, shake or use a soft long bristled brush or small nylon broom to gently remove as many bees as possible. Seal the bucket when you have finished this part of the exercise to prevent bees from returning to these nest components. When you get home, the honey pots can be squeezed and strained through a piece of fine mesh cloth or nylon stocking material to recover the tangy bush honey. This can later be fed back to the bees or used for your own consumption. In the latter case try to avoid the inclusion of pollen in the mix as this tends to taint the flavour of the honey.

The honey pots can be squeezed and their contents strained to recover the tangy bush honey. This can later be fed back to the bees or used for your own consumption. (Photo courtesy Bob Luttrell)

There will still be a lot of nest debris about, most of it covered with bees. Using the same methods you employed for the honey and pollen pots, remove as many bees as possible from the pieces of rubble before carrying this debris well away from the transfer site. Placing this rubble in full sunlight will also help to remove any remaining bees from it. The two main components of the old trunk may need further splitting to dislodge any bees in deep cavities. The fumes from a piece of cloth soaked in a little Tea Tree oil and jammed into inaccessible parts of the log can also help to drive out the remaining bees. A friend of mine simply turns each part of the log over, and then delivers an almighty blow with a sledgehammer to the outside before discarding each half well away from the site. Most of the bees are dislodged by the jolt and while they appear to be briefly stunned, they quickly recover and take off, usually in the direction of the new hive. It works for him and he has accumulated one of the largest collections of stingless beehives in Australia.

It becomes a waiting game now, so you can afford to relax and clean up. No doubt your hands will be sticky, not just from honey, but also from handling all the cerumen and tree resins in and around the hive. Methylated spirits will dissolve these resins, and a small spray bottle of it is a great aid to cleaning yourself up – followed by some soap and water and a towel. Aren't you glad you brought someone with you to carry all this stuff?

I usually fill in the time at this stage by putting the billy on the fire before sitting on the end of the log and beginning the tedious task of cleaning the sawdust and chips out of my socks and boots because I've forgotten to wear my sock protectors yet again. You may prefer to go away and come back a little before dark.

By dusk all bees that are capable of doing so should have found their new home. If your hive has an observation panel take a quick peek inside. Hopefully the brood area will be covered with bees, all busy trying to protect, stabilize and secure the most precious component of their nest.

Seal up the hive entrance with a ventilated plug or with some porous material to allow them some ventilation on the way home. A small section of fly screen mesh, or nylon stocking material, placed over the entrance and taped around the edges works quite well, as does a twist of shade cloth pushed into the entrance hole. Don't forget the drain holes in the bottom. A small twist of shade cloth in these will confine the bees, but still allow the honey to drain through.

Now while you carry the hive carefully back to your car, get your mate to remove the steel picket and collect the chainsaw, wedges, crowbar, sledgehammer, beach umbrella and bucket of honey. Just make sure he doesn't lose any of your smaller items of equipment in the long grass in the dark before you agree to shout him a beer on the way home.

11. Propagating Hives by the Splitting Method

The pioneers of stingless beekeeping, such as Dr Tim Heard, realized that a strong stingless bee colony could be split in half to produce two separate hives provided the half that missed out on getting the queen had at least one viable queen cell. Tim and others refined this process over time to the point where they could be assured of getting a high percentage of successful outcomes.

Dr Tim Heard splitting one of his Original Australian Trigona Hives (OATHs) (Photo courtesy Tim Heard)

The standard OATH box designed by Tim, and discussed earlier, is constructed in two equal halves to facilitate this method of propagation. At its most basic, the splitting method of propagation involves dividing the hive horizontally at its midpoint and equipping the old top part with a new empty bottom and the old bottom half with a new top. The bees are then left to furnish their new basement or attic depending on which side of the split they find themselves. Tim's hive design has proved itself over time, but that hasn't stopped others (including me) experimenting with different configurations. However, most of us recognise the soundness of Tim's initial concept and incorporate a feature that allows the hive (or at least the brood component of the hive) to be split in half. It remains the simplest and easiest way to multiply hives.

While the actual process of splitting a colony in half may seem a little brutal to the novice beekeeper the success rate is usually high – provided a few basic rules are followed.

First and foremost, you must consider the strength of the colony. Novices keen to increase the number of hives in their collection are sometimes tempted to undertake hive propagation prematurely and as a result may actually achieve the opposite result. Hives divided by this

View through part of the observation panel of an insulated tubing hive showing a hive brim-filled with **Trigona carbonaria** *bees. These bees are working amongst their brown cerumen pillars, struts and passageways shown still attached to the observation panel. This hive is ready to split.*

process suffer considerable damage and it is important that there are enough bees to not only repair the damage in both halves quickly, but also to protect the hives against invaders such as ants and the destructive syrphid and phorid flies.

It is generally accepted that a Trigona colony should weigh at least three kilograms before splitting is contemplated. You can get a rough idea of the strength of the colony by weighing the hive and deducting the weight of the empty box. However, it is not wise to rely upon this measure in isolation. Bee numbers may be depleted for some reason, and the hive's weight alone may not give a true indication of its strength.

Bee numbers need to be high, so if you don't have an observation panel on your hive you may need to open it up to conduct a census of the inhabitants. If the bee population doesn't appear to be up to scratch it may be wise to simply reseal the hive and wait for another time.

While some experienced beekeepers split their hives in all but the very coldest months of the year, novices would do well to confine their hive divisions to spring and summer. Not only will there be more queen cells available within the brood mass during these months, but the colony will have some time to build up strength before the colder weather returns. Perhaps it might be timely to also dispel any perception that, being insects, our little bees can multiply like midges or mosquitoes in summer and recover their hive strength within days or weeks at most. We know it takes approximately 50 days from the laying of the egg to the emergence of the callow and a few more weeks after that before the bee reaches the foraging stage. With only one egg-laying female in the colony, hive growth can appear to be painfully slow to the novice keen to achieve rapid expansion. It could take two years or more before the two hives resulting from a split have reached the stage where they can be divided again.

The next most important consideration is the position of the 'advancing front' as discussed in section 4. As a quick reminder, the brood mass (usually located in the middle of the hive structure) goes through a slow, continuous cycle as new cells are added to the top and the older cells hatch out at the bottom. When the construction reaches its upper limit within the involucrum, the bees start at the bottom again in the space vacated by the emerging callows. This advancing front of new cells moves ever upward, usually in sync with the older brood hatching out above. Between the hatching cells above and the advancing brood below there is usually a small space. In **Trigona carbonaria** bees it is particularly distinct because of the regular spiral pattern of their brood. However, this division line between the old and new brood is also present in the brood mass of the other species, albeit in a less regular form.

Splitting a hive can be less traumatic for both the bees and beekeeper if the advancing front of the brood happens to be at the same level as the midway joint where the hive is designed to be separated into two equal parts. (Photo courtesy Lyndall Rosevear)

It is not uncommon for hives being rescued from natural locations to have a large brood mass. This particularly regular example of Trigona carbonaria brood in an old hollow log presented the beekeeper with an opportunity to create two artificial hives by dividing it in half. Note: in such cases it is also important to get a roughly equal division of the bee population if both hives are to survive. (Photo courtesy Lyndall Rosevear)

When a hive is divided, the brood tends to break apart at this natural line of division so it can be advantageous to time the split to coincide with the advancing front reaching the midline of the hive. To avoid damaging the brood, some keepers of Trigona bees will reassemble the hive if the advancing front is not at that point and put off the division until they judge the situation to be more suitable. Others simply divide the brood mass with a sharp knife or similar implement. The object is to split the brood into two roughly equal parts. Usually (but not always) the queen will remain in the half containing the advancing front, but provided there are queen cells within the brood of both halves the beekeeper can be reasonably assured that whichever half is queenless has the means to make another one.

As with most things, proper preparation beforehand can make the exercise go more smoothly on the day and enhance your chances of success. If the entrance of the hive is round, then one thing I do is to slip a very short length of thin walled plastic tubing into the entrance a week or more before doing the split. Its purpose will become more apparent later on, but basically it is a device I use to transfer some of the old entrance scent to that part of the split which receives the brand new entrance. The black stuff about 12 to 13mms in diameter, which is sold for garden irrigation purposes, is ideal. The intention is to create a removable entrance 'sleeve' or lining, so just a 1 cm length pressed in until it is nearly flush with the outside of the hive box should be plenty. If it is too big in diameter it can be cut down the side and folded over itself a little. However, if your hive's entrance is particularly small you will need to be careful that this sleeve doesn't restrict access and ventilation too much.

An empty box with the same dimensions as the one about to be split is needed. It is possible to join boxes of different designs, including round ones to rectangular ones, by using a ply 'baffle' board between the two halves, but the result is often an ungainly looking structure. The floor of the new bottom section needs to have at least two, but preferably four, small holes to drain away most of the honey that will inevitably be spilled. Prepare yourself mentally for the fact that it is inevitable that you will drown and squish a number of bees. Just like the bee rescue mentioned in section 10, your first split will be a traumatic event for both you and the bees. But with a little care, you and both hives will come through okay.

Pick a fine day and try to undertake the split when the bees are most active. The starting time is not so important during warm weather, but make sure you can complete the exercise by 4pm at the latest so that the bees have a good chance to settle down before nightfall. Having said that there are a few experienced people who successfully split hives at night, but this is not recommended for the novice beekeeper. It is important to have all the tools you might possibly need within easy reach and for you and any assistants to be suitably attired as outlined in the bee rescue section. As also mentioned in that section you will need to protect the brood against exposure to full sunlight.

The "operating theatre" has been prepared, and the instruments are assembled, so it's time for the "surgery". Using a large screwdriver or similar tool, begin to prise the hive apart. It will be well secured with cerumen but, as the two parts begin to separate, peer inside to inspect the brood. If it is breaking naturally at about the midpoint of the hive, all is well and good. If not you will need to insert a long-bladed knife to divide the brood mass into two equal parts before fully separating the halves. Don't waste time looking for the queen after the hive comes apart, but if you happen to see her make a note of which half she is in. Put the empty top on the old bottom half, and put that hive to one side for the moment. That's the easy part done.

Now you'll probably have your hands full at this point. The top half of the hive will be drizzling honey over everything including you, the bees will be as angry as hell and your surgical assistants may want to drop the shade cover they are holding and run because they wouldn't wear protective clothing, and the bees are up the legs of their shorts. On top of this, if you have not already done so, you need to consider installing something at the midpoint to support the contents of the top half of the old hive before you put the two halves together. If you don't it is likely that the hive structure inside the top half will slump, especially in hot weather when the cerumen softens, drowning bees and brood and putting paid to that part of the split.

One solution is to install a piece of wire mesh or netting across the top of the empty bottom half. However, this often has the effect of later dividing the box, with the bees filling in the mesh with sheets of cerumen. They will store honey and pollen on both sides of the divide, but may refuse to extend the brood structure through the mesh, which can make future splits impossible. Cutting the centre out of the mesh can help to alleviate this problem, but a simpler solution is to stretch two lengths of masking tape across the width of the bottom half to cradle the contents of the top half before you lower it gently into place. This tape causes the bees no problems and later becomes incorporated into the hive's structure.

Now the two hives are assembled your fidgety assistants can retreat to a safe distance, but you still have a bit of work to do. Taping around the midpoint of both new hives not only helps to keep the halves together until the bees can properly seal up the joins with cerumen, it also helps to prevent the entry of pests such as the larvae of the syrphid and phorid flies. These flies, together with some species of ants, are the bane of stingless beekeepers and constitute a serious threat to newly split hives.

Install the new hive containing the full top half in the place occupied by the original hive. The other hive can be placed immediately alongside or even on top of the first one. Whatever placement method you choose ensure your ant barriers are up to scratch, because some species are opportunistic and may take advantage of the fact that the bees' natural defences are in disarray.

It is more than likely the returning bees will now favour one hive over the other and usually they will focus on the hive with the old entrance. This is where the little trick with the entrance sleeve, mentioned earlier, comes into play. Pull it out of the old entrance (you might need pointed nosed pliers if the bees have really stuck it in place) and slip it into the new entrance in the empty bottom box. This can help to ensure a more even distribution of bees between the two hives. Alternatively, if you are working with a species of bee that adorns its entrance with cerumen or resin you could scrape some off, warm it slightly and then try to mould it around the new one, but, I find the entrance sleeve an easier and less sticky solution. If, after a couple of days, you notice a greater concentration of bees in one nest than the other switch the hives about so that the returning foragers will return to the weaker hive. An observation panel in your hives can be of assistance at such times.

Instead of leaving the hives together you may prefer to move one at least a kilometre away. In this case, it is suggested that you relocate the one with the old bottom half because its contents are more stable than the one with the brood suspended in the top.

If a split has been done correctly the colony will quickly recover from the disturbance. Bees will soon be out foraging as normal, returning with stores for the hive like this pollen-covered worker which has been visiting palm inflorescences. On watch is a guard bee that is busily doing her duty.

If you favour a fairly large diameter entrance on your hive (12mm diameter or wider) as I do, you might consider temporarily closing it down by a third or so with a blob of cerumen or Blu Tac. The bees often take this step themselves under such circumstances. They may even close up the entrance completely. This is part of their defensive strategy after such upheavals, so don't go clearing the entrance out with a screwdriver or the like. The bees are unlikely to suffocate, and they will open for business again when they are ready.

There is one aspect of concern about splitting the brood mass horizontally at the advancing front that needs to be mentioned. Perhaps you have recognised already that, particularly when the advancing front is at the midline at the time of the split, one of the new hives gets all the young brood, while the other gets the more mature part of the brood mass. The high success rate achieved with this horizontal splitting process suggests that in most cases this is not a significant problem. Perhaps this is because the old queen usually stays with the new brood, but one could speculate that if she happened to wind up in the half with the older brood during the chaos created during the split, then it might be a long time before a queen cell hatched out in the other colony. Could this affect the chances of survival of the colony with younger brood? Only experimentation and observation over time will tell. Maybe one of the standby virgin queens mentioned in section 5 seizes her chance to reign in such circumstances.

One innovative beekeeper uses a different splitting method and as a consequence doesn't have to worry about that aspect at all. Les Felhaber of Rockhampton has designed a long, horizontal hive, which splits vertically through the middle section that houses the brood. The division is achieved by passing a hot wire down through the joint between the box halves and of course right through the brood as well. Each half is then furnished with a new empty box to the right or the left as appropriate. This process ensures both new hives resulting from the split has brood with the same age profile throughout.

Les Felhaber of Rockhampton has designed a long, horizontal hive, which splits vertically through the middle section that houses the brood.

12. Propagating Hives by the Eduction (Budding) Method

Educe, v.t., to draw forth or bring out; elicit; develop. [Source: The Compact Macquarie Dictionary, 1994].

While I certainly don't claim to have discovered the eduction method of propagating stingless beehives, I can take the blame for coining the term 'eduction', now often used for the process. By the time I was introduced to stingless beekeeping, a few of the real pioneers had for some time been connecting empty hive boxes to colonies in trees or walls with a piece of tubing, and were finding that occasionally they could obtain new hives in this way.

Becoming intrigued by this process, which nobody seemed to have a name for at the time, I recalled the rather obscure verb 'educe', noun – eduction. For want of a better term I started referring to the method by that name and it sort of caught on, especially with stingless beekeepers in south-east Queensland. We have since learned that scientists use the word 'budding' as the technical term for such a process.

The name is not important but the process is, because it provides a very useful alternative to splitting as a method for propagating stingless beehives. It is also the only method whereby a new hive can be drawn forth, or developed from, an existing nest in a tree or wall that can't be felled or demolished. Another benefit is that the original nest remains intact, which usually means that eduction can be repeated year after year.

However, the method need not be confined to the role of extracting a new hive from a parent colony located in an immovable object. While it requires considerably more time and patience than the splitting method, eduction can also be used as a means of propagating artificial hives. I now use this method extensively to propagate my beehives, not only because I consider it to be less disruptive to the bees, but because it also offers certain other advantages that will be revealed in this section.

Eduction can be used as a means of propagating artificial hives. The empty hive at the front has been connected to the parent hive by means of black plastic tube. The tube has been covered with shade cloth to keep it cool in the midday sun and to disguise the old entrance from the bees.

Part of the time involved, and patience required, for a successful eduction attempt, revolves around the preparatory work. While the time of the day and even the time of the year are not as important for this process as they are for the splitting method, there are some aspects that are common to both propagation techniques.

Firstly, similar criteria apply in assessing the parent hive's suitability for propagation. Eduction should not be attempted unless the parent colony has a good population of bees and weighs 3kg or more in the case of *Trigona* bees. Now, that's pretty easy to assess in one of your artificial hives. Peer through the observation panel and check out how many little white faces are peering back at you before weighing the hive and deducting the known weight of the empty box. But how do you make an accurate assessment of the strength of a nest in a wall or large tree? You can't, you can only make a guess based on the activity at the entrance, the amount of resin around the entrance and the noise level coming from the hive. This latter mentioned sign is the least reliable indicator of a colony's strength. Sometimes even the strongest colonies will only have a few bees humming in the choir at a particular time.

Having assessed that the parent colony is suitable for eduction, you might think that it is now simply a matter of drilling a hole in the back of your new empty hive and connecting it to the entrance of the old nest with a piece of tubing; thereby forcing all the bees to travel through the empty box in front to get out. Well that's the basic idea of course, but there's a whole lot more that needs to be done before you can expect the bees to make a home in your new hive.

As with the splitting process, eduction will go more smoothly if the bees' identifying scent can be transferred to the entrance of the new hive. The pheromones the bees deposit in and around the entrance act as a guiding light to their front door. Being able to easily relocate this beacon helps to minimize the disruption you are about to cause by moving their door.

Before we come to how this practice might be applied to a nest in a tree or wall, let's examine how you intend to attach your empty box to the parent colony. I've made this easy for myself because all my units (they're round plastic tubes so I can't really call them 'boxes') have both front and back entrance holes made from plastic tubing, having an internal diameter of about 15mms. This means that the black plastic tubing sold in most hardware stores for home garden irrigation purposes fits snugly inside. As described earlier, in the section on 'splitting', a 1 cm length of this stuff is also ideal for making a removable entrance sleeve, which is my preferred method for transferring entrance pheromones to the new hive. If the front entrance to my hive is to be in the bottom half of the unit, I then put the eduction tube at the back in the top half or vice versa. Forcing the bees to traverse this longer, staggered course seems to facilitate their acceptance of the new hive, perhaps because they see it as a new room rather than as just an extended hallway to their real home.

Whether you choose black plastic tubing, or decide to cut a piece out of the garden hose, it is important that whatever you use to connect the two hives is completely opaque. Light entering through the walls or ends of the tubing will disorient the bees as they try to travel from their hive to the new box. If you have any doubts about light getting through it, bind the tubing with black electrical tape or something similar. However, the use of dark coloured tubing (or binding) can present a problem itself in that it can become excessively hot if exposed to the sun during the middle of the day. To overcome this problem wrap the connecting tube in a small piece of shade cloth and extend this back to cover the old entrance. This not only keeps the tubing cooler but also helps to disguise the original entrance from the bees.

The idea is to keep the connecting tubing as short as is practical while making sure one end is properly fixed into the entrance of the parent hive and the other into the rear of your empty box. These connections need to be secure because the two hives are likely to remain joined for quite some time, several months in some cases. That's all very well when the parent colony is in another artificial hive with a nice round entrance of the right diameter to plug the tube into, but what about that tree or wall we mentioned earlier? Well here you might need to get a bit inventive, but perhaps I can assist with some of my ideas.

If the colony has a small, round entrance in a solid tree, you may be able to widen it by simply drilling it out to match the size of your tubing with a cordless drill or an old fashioned brace and bit. There's no need to go too deep, a centimetre or two should be sufficient. It is preferable to do this preparatory work a few days before making the actual connection. After drilling the hole insert an 'entrance sleeve' and leave the colony alone until the bees have settled down again and coated the new entrance with their resinous material and, more importantly, with their pheromones.

Concrete block or brick walls can be a more difficult proposition, because not everyone will appreciate their architecture being defaced by an enthusiastic beekeeper with a hammer drill. In these cases, or where an entrance in a tree is large or irregular, try affixing a small black plant saucer or even a black funnel over the entrance. The plant saucer will need to be drilled beforehand to take the tubing you intend to use, but the tapering funnel may allow you to simply plug the tubing onto it. How you affix these items to the wall or tree will depend on the circumstances. A long screw or even a nail can sometimes be used, but if you have to resort to glues avoid the strong smelling toxic ones. Gaps can be filled with Blu Tac or some other non toxic, putty like material. Blu Tac, by the way, is surprisingly durable in the weather, but the bees will usually attempt to chew their way through it. Sandwiching a small piece of aluminium foil between layers of the Blu Tac will stop them in their tracks.

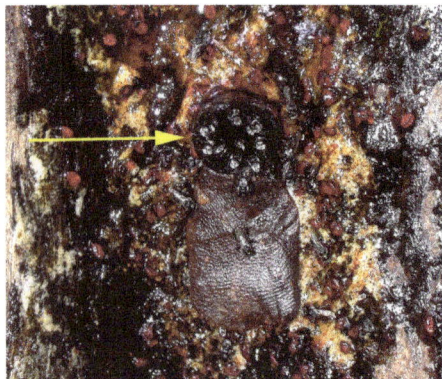

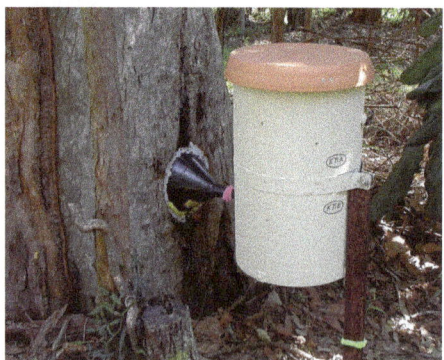

*These 4 photos show the steps involved in connecting an artificial hive to a standing tree containing a strong **Trigona carbonaria** colony. 1. The entrance sleeve (arrowed) has been in place for some time and is now well accepted. 2. The dead timber surrounding the entrance to the nest is being levelled to take the black funnel. 3. Securing the funnel in place with flat headed nails. Note that Blu Tac has been used under the edge of the funnel to provide a seal. 4 Empty hive is now in place and the eduction attempt has commenced. Note the ant barrier around the star picket supporting the hive. A similar barrier can just be seen wrapped around the connecting tube behind the hive.*

Unfortunately eduction is not an exact science but it appears that, if conditions are right, we can sometimes trigger the natural hive reproductive process. What "buttons" we need to press, at what time, and in what order are by no means certain, but getting as many details right as we can enhances our chances of achieving a spontaneous eduction.

There is another step that you can take at this point which, while not essential, does facilitate the acceptance of the new entrance by the bees. Move your old hive back a bit and position your new empty box in exactly the same spot as that previously occupied by the parent hive. But what if your parent hive is up against the back fence and can't be moved back? This is part of the preparation mentioned earlier. Move the parent hive forward a week or two beforehand, so that it can be moved back later to make room for the new hive in front. Obviously you can't do this if the parent nest is in a wall or tree, in this case the bees will just have to reorient themselves to the new entrance in front of their old one as best they can.

Prior to making the umbilical connection between the two hives, remove the entrance sleeve from the old one and slip it into the front of your new box. Alternatively transfer some resin from the old entrance to the new as outlined earlier. Returning foragers will recognise the scent of their old front door and will usually go straight inside. They will get quite a shock when they enter the front parlour and find a big empty space devoid of all their cerumen furniture. Some may even exit again to check if they've come home to the right address, but within an hour or two most will have accepted the new arrangement. I mentioned before that the time is not so important when it comes to setting up the eduction connection. However it is best not to leave it too late in the day. Give the returning bees a chance to reorient themselves before nightfall, especially during the cooler months of the year.

I have used the eduction process to establish a number of new nests in my round tubing hives from a parent colony housed in a modified OATH box.

You have probably recognised by now that another advantage of the eduction technique is that it is not dependent upon the "parent" and "daughter" hives involved being of the same design. For example, over the past few years I have used this method to establish a number of new hives in my round tubing hives from a parent colony housed in a standard OATH box. However, regardless of how simple or ornate your new box might be, I once again recommend that an observation panel be incorporated into its design. This feature is pretty much essential to the success of the eduction process.

Let's move ahead now to when the hives have been connected together for two or three weeks and the bees are using the new entrance like they never knew any other. What has happened inside the new box in that time? That's impossible to predict, so let's take a peek through the observation panel. Some colonies will accept the new box readily and start gluing up all cracks and joins almost at once. Others may just use it as a temporary rubbish tip for their discarded cocoon casings for some time. However, sooner or later, if the parent hive is strong, or crowded enough, the bees will begin making an unusual structure out of coarse cerumen behind the new entrance. I call it a 'draft baffle' because I initially thought it was designed to control the flow and temperature of the air entering the hive as part of its air conditioning system. However, it might be just as appropriate to assume that it is part of the hive's internal defences, or perhaps a combination of both these functions. Often a similar structure is built on the opposite wall as well, where the connecting tube enters the new hive.

Honey and pollen pots will progressively begin to make their appearance on the walls, accompanied by varying amounts of filamentous structure and sometimes thicker wavy layers of cerumen. When we see this activity we can speculate that either the bees have run out of pantry space in the parent hive and have decided to store their excess food in their new annexe, or we have triggered the mechanism that causes them to provision a new home for a daughter hive.

At this stage, if your stars and some other factors are in alignment, brood cells will magically appear and a new hive is born. There is still some debate as to whether the old queen wanders into the daughter hive and begins the new colony, hive, or if a virgin queen leaves the old nest via the tube, mates and returns to the new hive to begin her own colony. My observations have convinced me that it is the latter situation, and this is in line with my speculation that at times we can trigger natural hive reproductive impulses with the eduction process. Those other factors I mentioned include the strength of the parent hive, the time of the year, the condition of the season and probably a number of other aspects we have yet to discover.

Hives established by a spontaneous eduction, which make it through their early infancy, seem to become particularly vigorous within a relatively short period of time. Perhaps this is because the hive has been established by a more natural process, without duress and due to the presence of a young queen nurtured in a largely undisturbed colony.

Unfortunately, for every silver lining there's a cloud, so now for the bad news. Spontaneous eduction can be a hit and miss proposition – with a lot more misses than hits. A success rate as low as one in twenty attempts can be expected in poor seasons.

But don't give up on this process just yet – there's some good news as well. If spontaneous eduction has not occurred within a reasonable period of time (and this may mean several months in the cooler parts of the year) you can then switch to what I call 'assisted' or 'induced' eduction.

Now the purist will probably argue that induced eduction is just a modified form of hive splitting. Well maybe it is – and maybe it's not – I'll let you be the judge. It does involve seeding the new hive with a segment of brood containing a queen cell from an established colony. This is done after the new hive has been provisioned by the bees and is usually best undertaken during spring and summer when queen cells are more plentiful within the brood mass of the parent hive. Significantly, the brood to be seeded into the new hive does not have to be taken from the hive to which it is attached. The bees will accept brood from any hive of the same species. This enables the beekeeper to exercise some control over the parentage of the new hive, at least for the female line.

It is noticeable in a large collection of beehives that despite being given identical conditions, some colonies will do much better than others. Utilising the queen cells from these stronger colonies to start new hives enables the beekeeper to maintain a vigorous strain of bees. Nature herself, through the testing elements of the bees' mating flight, selects the strongest drone from the swarm for the male role in the nuptial proceedings.

This brood selection aspect is another advantage offered by the eduction process. Often it is possible to extract enough brood comb with queen cells from one strong colony to seed 2, 3 or sometimes even 4 hives set up for eduction. The colonies behind these seeded hives are not disturbed in any way. They now merely serve as 'surrogate' parent hives, providing support and defence of the introduced brood and ultimately to the foreign queen that hatches out.

Unlike spontaneous eduction, the chances of success with assisted eduction are quite good, probably in the order of 60% to 70%. In any case, the technique lends itself to repeated attempts, so provided you have an adequate supply of brood from other hives, you can keep trying until you and the bees get it right. In my experience, this should rarely exceed two attempts.

Before we move on to the trickier bits of the eduction process, perhaps I should just mention three other aspects relevant to brood transfers:

1. Try to transfer the more mature brood cells from the donor colony. With a little practice these are recognizable in all species, but they are particularly obvious in *Trigona carbonaria*

*A section of mature **Trigona carbonaria** brood ready for seeding into a new hive. Note the presence of three queen cells (A) near the centre of the photograph. Close inspection may also reveal the eyes of the developing embryos (B) just visible through the tops of the cells.*

because they are distinctly lighter in colour. This is due to the outer wax having been removed by workers in anticipation of the emergence of new bees. Given that it takes approximately 50 days from the time the egg is laid until the young bee emerges, selecting the more mature brood for transfer can help to reduce the time taken to establish a new hive.

2. It is difficult to advise just how much brood should be seeded into the new box, but more is better than less. It is a balancing act between ensuring that the recipient hives get enough brood cells to give them a good start and not depleting the parent hive to the extent that it could be put at risk.

   It appears that the callows, which emerge in the new box from the transferred brood before the young queen emerges, are essential to the success of the process. Queens will emerge from queen cells transferred in isolation, but without the support of their young wax producing, cell making siblings they usually do not advance to the egg laying stage.

3. To reduce the risk of fighting behaviour, try to remove as many adult bees as possible from the piece of brood about to be transferred. A soft bristled paint brush or the like can be helpful in this regard, especially if you haven't got enough puff to dislodge them with a strong blow.

   Check out developments every few nights through your observation panel. New brood cells should start to appear sometime after the queen cell hatches out. Be patient, as it may not happen immediately. Weather conditions and other factors may delay the mating flight considerably. But it could just be that the seeding hasn't worked on this occasion and you will need to try again.

However, let's assume that things have gone according to plan, and the budding you have induced is just starting to develop into a new hive. We can also reconverge our discussion with the development of the hive, mentioned earlier, that resulted from the spontaneous eduction; for, at this point, both daughter hives have reached the same stage and from hereon the same conditions apply.

This is also where things get a little tricky. Separation of the parent and daughter hives is, of course, our ultimate aim, but the timing of this separation can be critical. If separated too early, when the daughter hive has only a few brood cells, it may fail. Remember it will be about fifty days before those first few cells start hatching out and quite a bit longer before the bees reach the foraging stage. Most of the mature workers in the daughter hive will have died before the new bees emerge leaving the hive weak and undefended. On the other hand, leaving the hives connected for too long can be equally disastrous because we virtually have two queens in the one hive. In my experience, the old queen usually prevails in this circumstance and, either directly or indirectly through her workers, disposes of her royal rival. You may suddenly notice that you can no longer find the new queen on her little patch of brood and there are no new empty brood cells being constructed. Eventually the new brood will all hatch out, but no new brood will take its place. Macbeth's treachery pales by comparison with the royal murders in stingless beehives.

By careful management and monitoring of progress through the hive's observation panel, the beekeeper can help to avoid such a tragedy befalling the new colony. As mentioned previously, night inspections with a torch are preferable to inspections during the day. Not only does the absence of sunlight reflections off the glass enhance visibility but, as the foragers are all home, a better assessment of the hive's strength can be made. For extended observations, a red lens fitted to your light source will cause less disturbance to the bees – but maybe not to your neighbours. New hives started by the eduction method, which are still in this early stage of development, rarely build an involucrum around the brood, so the construction of these cells can be easily monitored. Usually the queen can also be seen on the brood and, if you are lucky enough, you may even observe the egg laying process. Watching a newly educed hive develop through the observation panel can add a new dimension to your enjoyment of keeping stingless bees.

Normally, the parent and daughter hives will live in harmony for the first week or two after the new queen starts laying. However, this is by no means a precise timetable and you will have to use your own judgment to some extent. As a rough guideline, the new queen can usually be expected to create a brood mass about the size of a ping-pong ball before friction between the two royal families results in murder or war. But a brood mass of this size may not be enough to sustain the new colony if it was separated at this stage. Besides, it will be too long before it starts hatching out. A successful eduction is, therefore, dependant upon the beekeeper being able to reduce the tension between the two colonies without separating them until the time is right. This can be achieved by cutting or drilling a hole in the connecting tube as near as practicable to the entrance of the parent hive. You may have to reposition any shade cloth covering you have in place to allow the bees from the old hive to use this alternative entrance.

Col Webb, a respected south-east Queensland beekeeper, uses a more sophisticated approach. He incorporates a plastic 'tee' piece in the tubing when he connects the hives. The spare segment of the 'tee' is blocked off until he judges the time is right to provide the parent hive with a side door.

Providing this extra entrance seems to relieve the pressure on the parent hive. Most foragers will still continue to return to the new hive, but the old hive will set up guards at the new entrance, and some bees will start coming and going without traversing the hive in front. This arrangement can then be left in place for many weeks if required while the new hive builds up strength. Eventually, one or both of the hives will build a dividing wall within the connecting tube and this is a good indication that the hives can be safely separated.

It is not necessary to relocate one hive immediately after separation. They will usually continue to live in harmony for quite some time if left in close proximity. Sometimes I turn the parent hive around 90 or 180 degrees after the separation to encourage more foragers to return to the new hive, but I have not established that this procedure is of any real benefit. If you do want to move one of the hives away, it is preferable to relocate the parent hive to avoid disturbance to the weaker new hive. However, if the parent colony is in a tree or wall it is the new hive that has to go. Another advantage of the eduction process is that, if the parent colony is still strong, there is nothing to stop you hooking up another empty hive in front and repeating the process.

13. War & Peace

Stingless they may be but, regrettably, our native social bees are not always peaceful. Occasionally a large fighting swarm will assemble and the combatants will fight to the death. These are not all short-lived skirmishes either; sometimes the encounter will persist for days with the swarm reforming each morning to do battle in their war of attrition. The ground may be littered with hundreds or even thousands of worker bees locked together in combat from which very few will survive. This miniature battlefield is made even more gruesome by the sight of teams of the ever-present ants dragging away the grounded and therefore mortally wounded bees to their own nests while the dogfights continue overhead. Such battles are a windfall for these opportunistic scavengers regardless of the outcome of the aerial warfare above.

*Aerial combat as a fighting swarm does battle in front of a **Trigona carbonaria** hive. Here an empty hive has been placed on top of the hive under attack in a vain attempt to distract the attacking force.*

Stingless beekeepers are perplexed by this fighting activity which can rapidly reduce the foraging strength of the hives involved. Fighting swarms can occur unexpectedly at any time of the year, although they are usually more prevalent in the warmer months. To add to the mystery it appears that while stingless bees are widespread throughout the warmer regions of the globe, there are relatively few reports of such fighting behaviour outside Australia. The Trigona species are the most belligerent, but on occasions our *Austroplebeia* bees will also engage in this aggressive and destructive behaviour.

I should also hasten to add that fighting swarms are not confined to collections of artificial hives. They have also been observed in naturally occurring colonies. By the way I am reluctant to use the term 'apiary' when referring to a collection of stingless bee hives because that word is obviously derived from the scientific term for the honeybee species ('Apis'). Perhaps we should coin the word 'Trigonary' as the collective term for our stingless beehives; but I digress from my dissertation on bee warfare.

Given our busy lifestyles and work commitments, the first indication stingless beekeepers may have that something is amiss is when they return home in the evening and find a carpet of dead and dying bees in front of their hives. By this time the remaining battle forces have retreated to their respective colonies for the night. In these circumstances the novice beekeeper might not connect the death toll with a natural event and assume that it is due to the effects of an insecticide or disease. If a close inspection of the dead bees reveals that most are locked together in pairs then you can forget about castigating your neighbour for his excessive use of lawn grub spray and be reasonably confident that a fighting swarm has taken place during your absence.

Those of us who have witnessed these fighting swarms first hand are usually more concerned about finding a way to separate the warring parties than making a detached scientific observation of the proceedings so there may be some variation in the description of fighting swarms amongst beekeepers. After seeing many of my own colonies engage in this behaviour over the years my composite impression is of a relatively tight formation of hundreds or sometimes thousands of bees forming up in front of one particular hive in the collection. Most of the individual bees within the swarm fly quickly in small circles and while the overall shape of the mass of bees may change a little in the wind the swarm usually stays within about 3 metres of the hive that is the focus of attention. On still days the buzzing sound produced by thousands of tiny rapidly beating wings is clearly audible. While it may be fanciful to say so, the combination of these aspects conveys the feeling of angry, aggressive intent.

As this aggression builds pairs of workers may lock together in flight and drop out of the air only to release each other and return to the swarm. This behaviour gives the impression that the opposing forces are testing out the strength of their enemies, but another suggestion put forward is that they are comrades in arms who have seized each other in error and have realized their mistake before any serious damage was done.

When the real fighting begins pairs of bees lock onto each other with their mandibles and fall to the ground in a savage wrestling match which usually results in the death of both of them. Bees appear to rain from the swarm and their bodies gradually build up on the ground below.

Stingless beekeepers are naturally keen to prevent or reduce the incidence of fighting swarms. However, to do this it is necessary to have some understanding of why they occur. In the past, the absence of definitive evidence led to wide ranging speculations and in some

*A carpet of dead **Trigona carbonaria** bees marks the aftermath of a large fighting swarm.*

cases to far-fetched ideas. Here we will confine ourselves primarily to discussing the two most popular theories for these clashes, 'territorial disputes' and 'home invasions'.

Amongst stingless beekeepers there is considerable support for the view that some fighting swarms arise out of territorial disputes, particularly when hives in a collection are positioned too close together. It is as though the bees from one hive resent the encroachment of other bees onto their turf. How much 'turf' a hive needs to feel secure is the subject of conjecture, but early theories suggested that hives should be positioned at least 5 metres apart. However, in natural settings, it is not uncommon to find two, three or even more colonies living within a single tree. It is also interesting to note that often a number of artificial hives in close proximity will live in harmony for years, but the introduction of a strange hive into their midst may suddenly trigger a major upheaval. On one occasion, while in the process of moving a Trigona carbonaria hive to another site, I left it briefly on the tailgate of my ute in order to install a steel post to position the hive amongst others already at this location. Within minutes a swarm

Scavenging ants remove the fallen from the battlefield.

formed up around the back of my vehicle with the bees showing interest, not only in the new hive, but also in some of the small cavities and dark areas on the ute such as the rubber stripping and the ends of roof racks. This type of activity is often reported as being associated with fighting swarms. At such times groups of workers will examine any holes or even dark spots they presumably mistake for cavities in the vicinity of a hive. Needless to say I did not feel the new colony would be welcome at this location and removed it without ever opening the entrance.

Hostilities may also erupt when one hive tries to take over another. Sometimes

*A **Trigona carbonaria** swarm (left) and an **Austroplebeia australis** swarm (right) attempt to invade the homes of their weaker neighbours.*

referred to as a 'home invasion' this usually involves a strong, belligerent colony attacking a weaker hive. As its name implies 'home invasion' involves a forced entry by the invading forces and presumably the installation of a new royal family. It has even been suggested that a young warrior queen intent on establishing her own colony might accompany the attacking swarm. As the size of the defending force dwindles an increasing number of bees from the dominant swarm land on the hive and begin forcing their way inside. Fighting pairs of bees may tumble from the hive entrance or be dragged out by a third worker as the battle continues inside the nest. A few bees will position themselves on tiptoe near the entrance and fan their wings vigorously, presumably releasing pheromones to call reinforcements to the action.

This aggressive behaviour may also cross the species barrier with at least one reported incident of a *Trigona hockingsi* colony invading and defeating a much weaker *T. carbonaria* nest. Unlike territorial disputes, home invasions are not always seen as disastrous events by the beekeeper. Often weak, barely viable colonies are transformed into strong hives following such an incident, despite the initial loss of bee lives. It doesn't pay to be too sentimental in stingless beekeeping. There is no compassion or pity in the world of insects - only survival of the fittest.

A recent scientific study used DNA 'fingerprinting' techniques to identify the participants in eight *Trigona carbonaria* fighting swarms. It showed that there were always workers from two or more colonies involved in the battle. Typically the swarm formed up close to the entrance of one particular hive and invariably bees from this nearby hive were present in the samples taken. The other bees involved may have been from a neighbouring colony or from some unidentified hive outside the sampling range. In 80% of cases the fighting pairs consisted of workers from these two colonies, but occasionally workers from the defending colony had fought each other to the death, probably mistakenly.

The study also showed that by tricking workers from one nest into returning to another could induce fighting swarms. The defending nest responded to this apparent invasion of foreign workers by mounting an aerial defence typical of

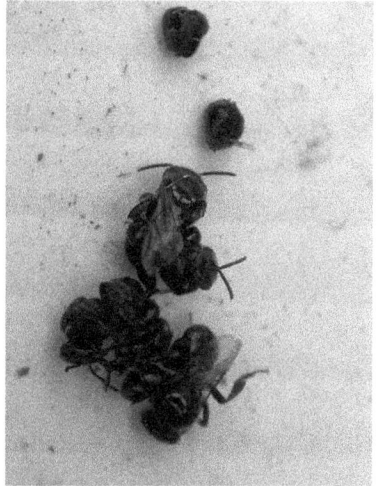

Austroplebeia australis workers fight to the death while in the background the heads of dismembered colleagues litter the battlefield.

fighting swarms. This data strongly supports the 'home invasion' theory, yet there are still many unanswered questions about this fighting behaviour. For example what factor stops two relatively equal colonies from continuing their war of attrition until the bitter end? In many cases a successful home invasion does not result from fighting swarms, yet the hostilities usually cease well before all the foragers are lost on either side. Do the combatants come to respect the relative strength of their opponent and agree to a cease-fire? Perhaps a more fundamental question is why is it better defensively to form up into a large flying swarm than simply strengthening the security of the entrance? By swarming out in great numbers at the first signs of possible invasion, is the defending colony displaying its strength? By so doing, are they trying to impress on the potential invader the foolhardiness of proceeding against it? Worker swarms have been known to disperse without fighting which may add some credibility to this proposition.

She may not look like a fighting machine, but at times **Trigona carbonaria** *workers will engage in savage aerial warfare with others of their own kind.*

These and other issues leave the subject open to speculation and experimentation by amateur beekeepers. Important discoveries have resulted from the observations of enthusiasts in many fields. As mentioned earlier this aspect can be one of the attractive features of this hobby.

Things we need to discover include how to identify when a hive is about to engage in fighting behaviour and then how to prevent it or at least stop it before it becomes too destructive. In this latter regard some techniques currently employed by stingless beekeepers include:

1. Hosing the swarm with a garden hose or sprinkler;
2. Spraying the swarm with a fine spray of water mixed with Eucalyptus or Tea Tree oil;
3. Placing a small piece of timber or something similar in front of the hive entrance to screen it from view;
4. Splitting the hive or hives involved;
5. Placing another empty hive in front of one or both of the hives involved;
6. Removing the hive under attack from the immediate area.

The more convenient measures listed as items 1 to 3 above usually only provide a brief respite, before battle is resumed. The remaining techniques often provide a more lasting solution, but are more difficult to apply and may not be practical in certain circumstances. In my experience the artificial feeding of hives whenever there is a noticeable drop in the natural nectar flow seems to lessen the incidence of fighting swarms. Having their food supply at home artificially maintained may reduce the incentive to attempt a takeover of the storehouse of another colony. It may also support an alternative proposition that hostilities might be exacerbated by the presence of too many idle foragers.

Having described fighting swarms in such vivid detail above, it is probably appropriate at this juncture to include a few words of reassurance for the novice beekeeper. While the outcome of fighting swarms looks dramatic and there is no doubt that the loss of so many foragers must weaken the hives involved it is unusual for such behaviour to result in the total loss of a colony.

Fortunately, peace reigns for most of the time in the stingless bee world and during these long periods of détente it is not uncommon to see another type of swarm build up and hover in the vicinity of a particular hive. Unlike the tight belligerent formation seen in fighting swarms these bees adopt a looser lazier pattern to their flight. For you see, fighting swarms are made up exclusively of female worker bees, but these more peaceful assemblies are drone swarms. Comprised entirely of male bees the participants of these swarms are only interested in making love – not war.

Presumably pheromones released by emerging virgin queens cause drones to assemble in large numbers in the vicinity of hives that may be intending to re-queen or to establish a new colony. Their patience seems to know no bounds. During fine weather these swarms will form up each morning and take up station in the same place for days or even weeks on end. Cruising aimlessly about in the warm sunshine while waiting for the object of their desire to emerge may seem fairly idyllic, but it's not all beer and skittles for these ardent suitors.

Those from more distant hives are forced to camp out if they don't want to miss the action next day and can be seen at night clustered on the thinner branches and twigs in the vicinity (see photo on page 20). When the queen finally emerges for her mating flight it is believed that she flies quickly upwards on a testing course to ensure that the weaker males fall by the wayside and that only a drone with the 'right stuff ' will father her future daughters. At such times the drones will be seen to leave their station en masse and sometimes after an initial wave-like action the swarm will climb steeply, only to resume its previous position some time later.

A stingless bee queen will engage in only one mating flight in her life and DNA evidence indicates that during that event she will mate with only one drone. However, the remaining bachelors in the swarm will continue their now futile patrol until predators and exhaustion take their inevitable toll.

14. The Good, the Bad and the Ugly

When you are as tiny and defenceless as a stingless bee, your chances of surviving to a ripe old age and dying of natural causes are pretty slim. Besides the cycles of floods, fires and droughts that are a feature of our bushland and which can threaten the whole bee colony, there are innumerable spiders, lizards, birds and predatory insects all too ready to snatch you from this mortal world. But not all these creatures present the same level of danger to a colony, and surprisingly there are a few that are directly or indirectly beneficial. Let's start with these.

The Good

Not too many people would describe termites as beneficial, but that's because we look at them from a biased human perspective. They're just a natural part of the bushland recycling process, but their indiscriminate attempts to recycle the wood in our Brick Veneer or Old Queenslander homes makes them decidedly unpopular with us.

In other parts of the world there are larger cavity making creatures such as Woodpeckers, but in Australia it is mainly termites and other wood-boring insects (and the fungi that accompany them) that create the tree hollows for so many of our bushland creatures. Unfortunately, these hollows are also sought after by some of the foreign invaders to our shores, including feral honey bees. In many areas of natural bushland, it is not uncommon to find more colonies of honey bees (*Apis mellifera*) that have gone wild than nests of our native stingless bees. The presence of these stinging invaders also has serious implications for other native tree dwelling creatures, including owls, parrots, possums, bats and gliders.

Termites with their insatiable appetite for cellulose create tree hollow homesites for many of our bushland creatures.

Stingless bees may occupy any suitable tree hollow, but they prefer those that have a relatively small entrance hole since it is easier for them to defend. Here the termites can be of assistance, because they create narrow tunnels to the outside world to allow the winged males and females of their own species to engage in their mating flights. These small holes widen over time through the processes of decay. Finally, a stingless bee scouting party discovers this passageway and decides the cavity within would make an ideal home for a new colony.

As discussed in previous sections, native bees use a particularly hard, tough cerumen mixture to wall off the area they require within the tree hollow. This protective structure is called the batumen. The termites may not have abandoned their workings when the bees take up residence, but have simply munched their way further up or down the heartwood of the tree. It is not at all uncommon to find a stingless bee colony abutting, or even completely surrounded by, an active termite nest. It is possible that, in such cases, the bees benefit from any warmth generated by the termites and other organisms of decay within the tree hollow.

Despite commonly being called 'white ants', termites are not ants at all, however, there are umpteen species of true ants in the Australian bush – many of which may also reside in our suburban backyards.

Here the foam insulating disk has been removed to show a 'Coconut-scented' ant colony sitting on top of the glass observation panel. A close inspection will not only reveal the mass of white ant eggs and larvae being attended by numerous small black adult ants, but also a number of winged male and female ants waiting to undertake their mating flights. Beneath the glass panel **Trigona carbonaria** *bees go about their business unperturbed by their upstairs neighbours.*

Having already mentioned about the need to protect stingless bee hives from ant attack, it may now seem contradictory to include them within the 'good' category. There is no doubt that a recently split or disturbed hive can fall victim to certain species of ants, but observations have caused me to question whether we need to tar all ant species with the same brush.

In natural situations, stingless bee colonies are invariably surrounded by ants with which they seem to have established some degree of peaceful co-existence. It is only when a bee colony is opened up, or disturbed in some way, that opportunistic species of ants take advantage of the situation. In my part of the world, it is the small, active black and brown models that cause the most trouble. On the other hand, some ants seem to live in reasonable harmony with my bees. I have a few hives in which the spaces under the roofs are occupied by colonies of tiny black 'coconut scented' ants, while others house nests of the much larger 'golden bum' ants, known in more polite circles as Golden-tailed Spiny Ants (*Polyrhachis ammon*) or a similar species. Polyrhachis ants are mainly nocturnal, and feed on the sugary secretions of scale insects and the like.

While the adult ants of some species can survive on sugary secretions, their young need protein food. It is possible that, in seeking to fulfil this need for protein, these ants do the bees a good turn by collecting the eggs or young larvae of syrphid flies or other bee predators deposited on or near the hive. This is just speculation, but there seems little doubt that a colony of ants would provide a deterrent to other bee predators such as lizards or spiders, or even larger invaders. I know I am reluctant to remove the lid of one hive because the ants are so numerous they immediately swarm all over my hands and arms and, while they do not sting, it is nevertheless an unpleasant experience. Despite the strength of the ant colony nesting on top of the observation panel of this hive, the bees on the other side of the glass are doing very well indeed.

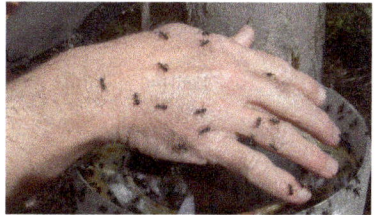

I am reluctant to remove the lid of one hive because the 'golden bum' ants are so numerous they immediately swarm all over my hands and arms.

In the absence of any noticeable harm to the bee colonies, I leave these types of ants in place. I kind of like the idea of two different types of social insect living in harmony within the same structure. If the ants actually provide a benefit to the bees within the hive in these circumstances, then that is a real bonus.

There is one more aspect that should be included in this 'good' category, and that is the fact that our stingless bees appear to be relatively disease free. They don't seem to suffer from any of the brood diseases experienced by the introduced honey bee.

*Every evening **Austroplebeia** spp. bees construct a security screen across their entrance.*

*Austroplebeia **australis** bees often construct a short entrance tube as a protection against invaders. This particularly symmetrical example protrudes from the entrance of a colony in a fire blackened log hive owned by Col Webb.*

The Bad

We'll start this segment with those paradoxical ants which, if I may paraphrase the saying about the Curate's egg, can be both good and bad. A strong, undisturbed colony of stingless bees can defend itself effectively against an attack by ants. The bees' static defences vary from species to species. *Trigona carbonaria* usually deposit sticky resin around their entrance, while *T. mellipes*, *T. sapiens* and *T. clypearis* build entrance tubes of varying lengths. The *Austroplebeia* species may sometimes build entrance tubes as well, but they are apparently more concerned about sneak attacks after dark. For this reason, every evening they construct a distinctive lacework screen of cerumen across their entrance and, provided the next day is fine, they take it down again in the morning, storing the component parts just inside their front door.

Stingless bees employ two main active defensive strategies. They bite and lock onto soft targets with their jaws, but as this is less effective against the harder bodied opponents like ants and beetles, they have devised an effective alternative technique. The bees repeatedly daub these invaders with small blobs of resin until they are rendered immobile. Large beetles that have inadvertently stumbled into a hive are often found entombed in resinous material within the hive structure.

The problem with ants usually arises when a hive is weak or has been disturbed in some way, and the bees' defences are in disarray. This may occur when the beekeeper is transferring a nest from a log to an artificial hive, or splitting a hive for propagation purposes. Despite what some treefellers may say, stingless bee colonies that disappear on the ground overnight have not simply found another home and moved off, they have been destroyed by ants and perhaps other predators. Remember, laying queens cannot fly and so colonies can't abscond like honey bees.

We've discussed ant proofing techniques previously, especially in section 9, but it is probably worthwhile to reiterate the need to put effective physical barriers in place, at least during the critical period which can extend out to several weeks for a bee hive that has been significantly disturbed. Hives mounted on steel posts are probably the easiest to ant proof by simply greasing or oiling the post. However, for really persistent ants, you may also need to carefully apply ant dust or sand to the area immediately around the base of the post. Other techniques include placing the legs of free standing hive supports in containers filled with water or suspending a natural log nest by a wire rope so that it is kept off the ground. When you've finished your ant proofing, step back and double check that those pesky ants can't bypass your blockade. Trim back any overhanging branches that may touch the hive or its support above your barricade.

Aside from the predators that attack our stingless beehives as merely opportunistic scavengers, taking advantage of a temporary breach in the bees' defences, there are a number of specific predators. One such insect that appears to specifically target stingless bee nests is referred to as the 'syrphid fly', and it is a nemesis of stingless beekeepers.

The syrphid fly is a wasp mimic. The antennae, which appear to branch from a single stem, are a distinguishing feature.

The Family Syrphidae is in fact comprised of a relatively large number of fly species and includes those harmless little Hoverflies that pause in midair amongst the daisies. Several members of the group are even regarded as beneficial, because they are effective pollinators and their larvae feed on aphids and the like. Unfortunately, the same cannot be said of the black sheep of the family, *Ceriana ornata*. This particular syrphid fly is quite distinctive in appearance. As mentioned in section 6, the casual observer could easily mistake one for a medium sized wasp or hornet, but it is a true fly and cannot sting. The unusual antennae, which appear to branch from a single stem, are a distinguishing feature.

Ceriana ornata is rarely, if ever, seen in areas where there are no stingless bee colonies. It may be that stingless bees are its primary host, but so little is currently known about this insect that such an assertion cannot be made with any degree of confidence. What is certain, however, is that this type of syrphid fly presents a real threat to stingless bee colonies, especially those in hives that have just been split or disturbed in some way. In such circumstances, it will appear from nowhere and begin laying its eggs adjacent to cracks or joins in the hive's surface. The larvae that emerge gain access to the hive through these unguarded entry points and begin feeding on the bees' honey and pollen stores. If they are in sufficient numbers they will reduce the internal hive structure to a sticky gooey mess resulting in the loss of the hive.

Syrphid fly larvae can reduce the internal hive structure to a sticky gooey mess resulting in the loss of the colony

This syrphid fly larva will soon progress to the pupae stage like those around it.

Prevention is easier than attempting a cure when it comes to a syrphid fly infestation. Strong, wellestablished hives are usually not at risk. They have the capacity to either prevent the entry of the fly's larvae, or to seek out and destroy any that slip past their security. It is when the colony's defences are in disarray that it is at most risk so, when splitting or rescuing hives, try to minimize the time the opened nest is exposed to these flies and other invaders. After the hives have been reassembled, carefully tape up any joins or other access points other than essential drain holes and wipe away any spilled honey on the hive. If you notice a syrphid fly depositing her tiny eggs on the hive by touching her abdomen down repeatedly then wipe the area with a cloth or sponge dampened with methylated spirits. It goes without saying that you cannot use insecticides, either in the form of aerosol sprays or surface coatings, to deal with these invaders. Temporarily reducing the size of the entrance with a piece of cerumen or Blu Tac can make it easier for the guard bees to defend their home until order is fully restored.

Include a fly swatter in your bee kit and don't be afraid to use it if a syrphid fly alights in a handy spot, even if it means sacrificing a nearby bee or two. A butterfly net fitted with a mesh that allows the bees to escape but not the much larger syrphid fly can be used even more effectively to reduce the number of these pests.

I have noticed that syrphid flies are strongly attracted to my solar wax extractor (pictured on page 99), a device I use for melting down cerumen recovered from rescued hives to obtain pure stingless bees' wax. It is likely that the scent of the honey associated with the cerumen is the chief drawcard for these flies. They lay their eggs all over this black box with a double glazed front without realizing that any larvae following the scent inside will be fried next day in the midday sun.

If syrphid flies are particularly bad in your area, you might consider making a device that works along those lines. A wide-mouthed plastic bottle with small holes punched in the upper part, or covered with a fine mesh to exclude bees, could be baited with honey and cerumen. If suspended nearby like a fruit fly trap it may help to lure some of the syrphid flies away from your hives. It should be periodically discarded or washed out with very hot water to destroy the fly eggs and grubs.

Second place on the list of undesirables goes to the phorid fly. Much smaller and less colourful than the syrphid fly, it resembles a hump-backed, overweight vinegar fly. Many flies in the Family Phoridae have rather unsavoury habits from our point of view. Common names including 'coffin fly' and 'drain fly' give a clue to their choices in cuisine. But it is unusual to find that all members of a family are undesirable types and that holds true here as well. In the USA one type of phorid fly is being used as a bio-control agent against the fire ant. Scientists are utilizing the tiny fly's reproductive cycle which involves parasitising individual ants as a means of controlling this invader.

*The humpbacked phorid fly is a little smaller than a **Trigona carbonaria** worker.*

Some overseas stingless bees suffer a similar gruesome fate. Bees are eaten from the inside out by larvae that develop from eggs injected by minute phorid flies. The phorid fly that is a problem for Australian beekeepers is a larger type, and its larvae have a taste for honey and pollen rather than bees' intestines. While less horrible for individual bees, the overall effects may be worse because destruction of the stores can lead to the death of the whole colony.

Unlike the syrphid fly, the adult phorid fly will enter the hive to lay its eggs. It seems to be able to evade the bees by its speed of movement. A badly infested hive will have many adult flies scuttling around very quickly on their legs alone. In fact, they seem to prefer running about to flying much of the time.

The distribution of this particular phorid fly appears to be somewhat patchy. In some areas, it is virtually unknown to beekeepers while in others it is a major pest, producing a similar result to the syrphid fly. Again, strong undisturbed colonies are not usually at risk. Not only are their defences more effective, but it is also possible that the greater number of bees within the hive makes evasion by darting about more difficult.

Experienced stingless beekeepers such as Alan Waters, Col Webb, Cec Heather and Bob Raabe, have developed an effective phorid fly-trap for installation within their hives. Adult flies are lured down a narrow tapering tube by the smell of honey

Resembling coffee grounds the countless bodies of dead phorid flies fill this container. This demonstrates the effectiveness of the traps used by Alan Waters, Col Webb, Cec Heather and Bob Raabe in the Ipswich area west of Brisbane.

placed at the bottom. This tube is fitted into an empty film canister where the flies are captured. The dimensions of the tapering tube are such that the bees are excluded.

Saving a hive that has been badly infested by either of these flies can sometimes be achieved by dramatic surgery. Cutting out the brood comb only and installing it in a clean hive with some unaffected honey and pollen stores from another source can prove successful, provided you still have a good population of bees. You will need to entice as many of these as possible into the new hive.

As for the old hive, you should ensure all traces of eggs and larvae have been removed before using it again. Scrape out as much of the old hive structure as you can. Spray the inside of the box with methylated spirits, which will not only kill the eggs and larvae it comes in contact with, but will also dissolve some of the resins within the remaining cerumen. Just remember that this stuff is flammable, so don't smoke or have naked flames around when you are spraying it about. Use a cloth or stiff brush to remove as much of the remaining cerumen as you can before placing the entire hive into a large, heavy duty black plastic bag and sealing it up tightly. Place this in full sunlight for a couple of days. The heat generated within should be sufficient to kill any eggs or larvae hidden away in joins or crevices.

There are other creatures that have the potential to infiltrate stingless bee nests and bring about their destruction. The introduced Small Hive Beetle, which is proving to be such a worry for honey bee keepers, is one such insect. Early indications are that the 'cerumen daubing' defensive technique employed by our stingless bees is proving effective in keeping them at bay. There is also a native hive beetle, but this is not believed to cause significant damage.

In other parts of the world bears, badgers and other honey loving creatures developed features and techniques that enabled them to break into bees'

Small Hive Beetle larvae ejected from a **Trigona hockingsi** *hive.* **Trigona** *bees not only deal with this foreign invader in this way, they also daub the adult beetles with cerumen until they are rendered immobile.*

nests. The absence of such creatures in Australia meant that our bees did not have to endure such attacks for much of their history. However, in more recent times, one foreign mammalian creature has emerged that has proven to be very destructive. Initially it only targeted individual colonies, but later it began to significantly modify its environment, wiping out entire habitats in the process. It also developed the ability to make toxic substances that it can emit through artificial means and so decimate the stingless bees and other insects adjacent to its own communal nesting sites.

I'm speaking of human beings of course but, as we are unique in being able to learn from our mistakes and reform our ways, perhaps we will not continue to present such a threat to our native bees and other beneficial creatures in the future.

The Ugly

A **Bembix** wasp at the entrance of her nesting tunnel which is provisioned with paralysed stingless bees. (Photo courtesy Bob Luttrell)

Had I not decided to confine the creatures in the 'bad' category to those that invaded the hive structure to bring about the colony's downfall, I would have included Bembix musca (a Sand Wasp) in their number. You might recall from section 6 that this handsome 'bee-like' wasp has an ugly side. It catches stingless bees on the wing and then paralyses them with its sting before storing them in its underground tunnels for its larvae to consume at their leisure. Up to thirty-five bees have been found in some tunnels and, as each wasp presumably digs several of these underground nest chambers, the predation rate on a colony from a number of these wasps can be quite high.

Another, much smaller wasp, belonging to the Braconid family seems to have adopted similar practices to those South American Phorid flies mentioned previously. It is so small and inconspicuous that its existence was not confirmed until late in 2006. The microscope or close up lens reveals its colourful appearance but this pretty and dainty facade belies the horror its presence holds for individual stingless bees. During the warmer months this tiny creature alights near the hive entrance to patiently and cautiously stalk on foot some of the nearby bees. When it finally gets close enough to one that presents an opportunity for ambush, it brings its ovipositor around beneath itself in order to quickly deposit its egg onto or perhaps inside the bee's abdomen.

The pretty daintiness of this tiny **Braconid** wasp belies the gruesome nature of its parasitism of stingless bees.

The minute size of this parasitic wasp is brought into scale when compared with its host, an adult **Trigona carbonaria** bee. The inset shows the actual size

The resultant larva develops within its host to the extent that it occupies almost the entire abdominal cavity of the bee. Surprisingly the infected bee remains mobile and some can still fly right up to the time the larva emerges. Even after the larva has emerged the bee may remain alive for a few hours, but it gradually weakens and all those observed to date have died as a result of the parasite. Immediately upon leaving its host the larva moves off actively, seeking a suitable place to undergo metamorphosis. Observations indicate that this takes place in the soil rather than within the hive.

The remaining 'uglies' can be categorized as those creatures that take a few individual bees, but are not usually a threat to the colony itself. Included amongst these are spiders, assassin bugs, dragonflies and even small lizards such as skinks and geckoes. Being listed as just ugly doesn't mean they should be totally ignored. Sometimes, their toll of individual bees can be high enough to adversely affect the foraging force of a hive. Spiders in particular have the potential to catch a lot of workers if their webs are strung in the bees' flight path. If practicable, clear these cobwebs away early in the morning before the bees start foraging. From time to time it may be necessary to humanely cull or relocate some of the other 'uglies' from around your hives if their numbers become excessive.

You may be wondering why the pollen mites referred to in section 8 have not been included in any of the above categories. Pollen mites are regarded as a symptom of hive malaise rather than being a cause of the decline. When the bee population drops to a point whereby the colony can no longer sustain the necessary level of hive maintenance and hygiene the mites invade or, more likely, are already present and simply increase dramatically in number. Strong healthy hives never show signs of pollen being dispersed by these mites.

An Assassin bug uses her antenna to gauge the distance to her victim that she will strike with her long proboscis.

The now common Asian house gecko is looking for an easy meal of stingless bees.

Whether lurking within the flowers or perched in their silken webs spiders are an ever-present danger to foraging stingless bees.

15. The Cadaghi Controversy

The Cadaghi (*Corymbia torelliana* but also known as *Eucalyptus torelliana*), is a medium-sized evergreen tree that occurs naturally in a small, well-defined area of tropical north Queensland centred on the Atherton Tableland. Despite this limited natural distribution, it is surprisingly tolerant of different climatic conditions and soil types. As a result, it has been widely planted by public authorities and private individuals in urban and rural areas of Queensland and New South Wales.

*A Cadaghi (**Corymbia torelliana**) planted in the Great Court, University of Qld, St Lucia Brisbane. Ironically a relief carving of a **Trigona carbonaria** worker bee features prominently on the archway to the Anthropology Dept in the background.*

The Cadaghi's creamy white flowers provide a bountiful harvest for stingless bees.

The Cadaghi is an attractive tree, especially when young, putting forth new growth covered in a pink to reddish fuzz. In very mature trees, long eucalyptus-type leaves replace the broad leaves of younger trees. It flowers profusely, usually in late spring to early summer. The creamy white, scented flowers provide a bountiful harvest for stingless bees and for all other creatures attracted to nectar and pollen.

It is not until a little later in the year that the controversial aspects associated with the Cadaghi arise. By December or January, the pollinated flowers have developed into round brownish 'gumnuts', which contain numerous flat seeds.

Coinciding with the seeds reaching maturity the gumnuts begin to exude a resin that is highly attractive to stingless bees, especially to the Trigona species; so much so that they appear to abandon all other resin sources and may even neglect normal foraging while Cadaghi's are producing these seeds.

A tree that produces abundant nectar and pollen when stingless bee colonies are expanding in spring followed by a ready source of resin for hive building in summer would seem to be ideal, but some stingless beekeepers consider *Corymbia torelliana* to be the greatest single threat to the well-being of their hives.

Eucalypts and related tree species expect a service from bees and other insects in return for the honey and pollen they provide. In most cases this is limited to carrying their pollen to other flowering trees to effect cross-pollination, thereby ensuring perpetuation and diversity. However, the Cadaghi requires quite a bit more and in the view of many beekeepers exacts a heavier toll than is necessary in the way it exploits stingless bees.

It is now widely believed that it uses the stingless bee as its primary agent for seed dispersal. This is no mean feat on the part of the tree. It may not be difficult to produce a substance that is highly attractive to insects, but bees gather nectar, pollen and resin, they don't have any use for seeds. But by fair means or foul the tree causes them to transport its seeds by the hundreds and thousands. It is probably an involuntary process on the part of the bees because it is commonplace to see returning foragers actively trying to free themselves of the unwanted burden of these seeds. The seed is just the right size to fit the pollen baskets, and it appears that while collecting the resin from within the gumnut the bees come into contact with the adjacent seeds. These then stick to the bees' legs with all the tenacity of Velcro. Sometimes, a returning forager will have a seed attached to each pollen basket and clearly is in overdrive trying to keep the load in the air. Maybe those bees that fall by the wayside with their burden provide a better result for the tree than those that actually make it back to the colony.

However, the tree's perfidy does not stop with the loss of a few foragers from exhaustion. The seeds

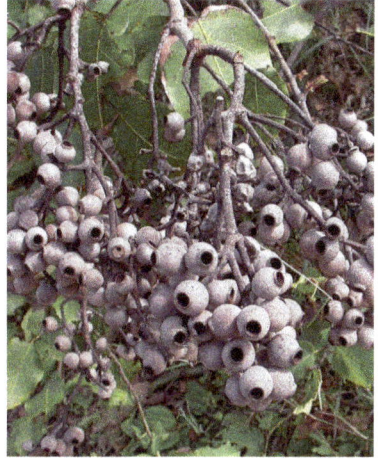

Cadaghi gumnuts – a mecca for stingless bees.

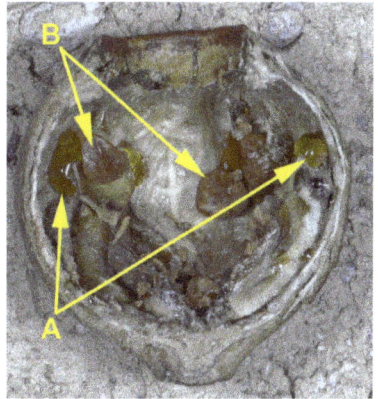

A dissected Cadaghi gumnut revealing (A) the sticky resin it exudes, which is so attractive to stingless bees and (B) the mature seeds ready to be dispersed involuntarily by the unsuspecting bees. (Photo courtesy Bob Luttrell)

Cadaghi seeds stick firmly to the legs of stingless bees foraging within the Cadaghi gumnuts. (Photo courtesy Bob Luttrell)

A Cadaghi seedling at the two-leaf stage. Under ideal conditions a carpet of seedlings may germinate in front of a stingless bee hive from seeds dropped by returning foragers or discarded from the hive during house cleaning operations. (Photo courtesy Helen Schwencke)

Corymbia torelliana *is easily distinguished from other trees in the Bloodwood group and from Eucalypts at all stages of their development. This Cadaghi shows the distinctive leaves and reddish fuzz on the stem and new growth that are features of young plants.*

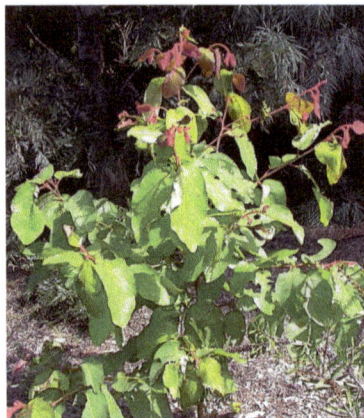

A flourishing young Cadaghi - the result of seed dispersal from the hive in the background.

accumulate around the hive's front door in such numbers that, in some cases, they can almost entirely block the entrance. There are beekeepers who assert that under the heat of the sun these seeds release fumes that can kill the colony but it is more likely that, by obstructing the entrance, the seeds interfere with normal ventilation resulting in suffocation or, because it occurs during the hottest part of the year, excessive heat build up overwhelms the colony.

It should be mentioned at this point that the effects of Cadaghi seeds are most noticeable in colonies of *Trigona carbonaria*. While this species is reported to extend as far north as the Atherton Tableland it is further south in Queensland and in northern New South Wales that *T. carbonaria* comes into its own as the most widespread stingless bee. In these areas it had no natural interaction with the Cadaghi tree. The tendency of *T. carbonaria* to use much more resin around the entrances of their hives than other species of stingless bees exacerbates the situation. This resin softens in the summer heat and under these conditions it can be almost as sticky as flypaper. The seeds from the returning forager's legs rapidly accumulate on this surface as shown in the accompanying photographs.

Despite the bees' efforts to dislodge the seeds before they enter their front door, most will be carried past the entrance and into the hive before the bees can discard them. Some of these are chewed up, others are left whole but, whatever their state, they become mixed with cerumen and incorporated into the colony's internal structure. The presence of Cadaghi seed destroys the smooth texture of the cerumen building material and is a real problem for beekeepers seeking to harvest this hive product. This distinctive cerumen and seed mixture may accumulate in such a quantity that it reduces the available living space within an artificial hive. Consequently, some beekeepers try to remove it after the Cadaghi season is over but this is a difficult and time consuming process. Others move their hives to Cadaghi free areas before the trees' seedpods mature, however, given the current widespread distribution of Cadaghis, these places can be difficult to find. It has also been reported that *T. carbonaria* will travel further than their normal range of about half a kilometre to obtain

Cadaghi resin, such is the attraction this substance holds for these bees.

The Cadaghi has one last nasty trick to play. It is reported that the resin the bees so avidly seek and collect at such a cost has a low melting point. The summer heat may be enough to soften it to the extent that the internal hive structure starts to slump. Colonies can be lost when the collapsing hive contents buries and suffocates the brood or queen.

Having said all this, it should be pointed out that not all stingless beekeepers are united in condemning the Cadaghi. Those not sharing the general concern point out that the tree's flowering period provides the bees with an abundant source of nectar and pollen. Also, some hives appear to cope with the influx of seed better than others and, where summer temperatures are not extreme, the resin doesn't seem to present a threat to these hives. A few beekeepers even report that their hives seem to progress rather than decline during the uptake of Cadaghi seed, though this may be simply because it coincides with the warmer weather when insect activity naturally increases.

There is also the interesting proposition that, if we accept that *Corymbia torelliana* employs stingless bees to disperse its seeds, then it would be contrary to the tree's interests to evolve features that lead to the loss of native bee colonies. If a parallel can be drawn with the pollination process that precedes seed production, then it is more usual for a tree to provide a benefit to the visiting bee rather than something deleterious. However, one shouldn't be too adamant about the validity of this theory. Could it be that the very reason such an adaptable tree was so limited in its natural distribution was because it got its seed dispersal strategy wrong by presenting a hazard to stingless bees outside that range?

The Cadaghi now has us modern humans to thank for its much greater area of distribution. Who could have anticipated beforehand that its widespread planting in public and private gardens would give rise to this controversy about its adverse effects on stingless bee colonies? Perhaps this should highlight to us the fact that, despite extensive research, it may be impossible to predict all the repercussions of relocating even native plants or animals outside their natural range.

*The entrance of this **Trigona carbonaria** colony living in an old Paperbark tree is heavily encrusted with Cadaghi seeds from recent plantings in a suburban parkland.*

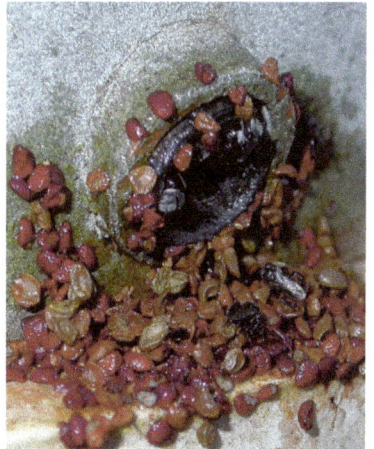

An artificial hive entrance encased in Cadaghi seeds in January.

16. Bee Friendly

Some recently developed cultivars of native plants such as this, called "Summer Beauty", not only produce a magnificent display of nectar rich flowers they are also suitable for the suburban garden. (Caution: if you inquire about the plant check to see that it is a nectar producer (some cultivars don't seem to be).

Being friendly to stingless bees, and for that matter to our entire range of native bees, means having regard to all their necessities for life. Growing suitable food plants is the most obvious requirement, but unfortunately it is beyond the scope of this book to include an exhaustive list of stingless bee attracting plants suitable for planting in your garden. The wide geographic distribution of native social bees and their eclectic tastes in flowers makes it more practical to just recommend a range of features to look for when shopping for new plants. Your local nursery can then suggest suitable plants which meet these general criteria that will grow well in your area. Bushcare or Landcare groups can also be of assistance in this regard and some Shire Councils have environmental programs that include providing advice on local native plant species.

A garden flowering with suitable plants will not only attract and help sustain our social bees, but will also enable you to enjoy the presence of some of Australia's solitary and semi-social bees. Many of these are quite striking in appearance, and interesting in their behaviour. The larger ones including the Great Carpenter Bees (*Xylocopa* spp.) and the Teddy Bear Bee (*Amegilla bombiformis*) have bulky furry bodies and their industrious buzzing can be heard from some way off. Another 'buzz pollinator', the lovely plump Blue Banded Bee (*Amegilla cingulata*) also moves noisily through the garden, sometimes showing a preference for blue or lavender coloured blossoms. Other solitary bees appear fleetingly, like living jewels, some with iridescent

A bee friendly garden will also enable you to enjoy the presence of some of Australia's beautiful solitary bees. Left: A Great Carpenter Bee feeding on Wisteria (photo courtesy Lee Byrnes). Centre: A Giant Carpenter Bee buried in a native Senna flower. Right top: A Blue Banded Bee also immersed in a native Senna blossom, displaying the distinctive blue bands on the abdomen that give this species its common name. Right bottom: Colour variations are not uncommon with various Blue Banded Bee species as demonstrated in this specimen with whitish bands on its abdomen. (photo courtesy Bob Luttrell) (centre and right top photos courtesy Frank Jordan)

Left: The furry Teddy Bear Bee taking its nightly nap with its jaws clamped to a twig often frequents Senna flowers (photo courtesy Frank Jordan). Centre: The leaves of the Senna are the food for the caterpillar of the beautiful Yellow Migrant butterfly (photo courtesy Helen Schwencke). Right: An irridescent-green Peacock Carpenter Bee on Tick Bush (**Kunzea ambigua**) (photo courtesy Frank Jordan)

colours such as the Peacock Carpenter Bee (*Xylocopa bombylans*). While we are taking the time to smell the roses, both figuratively and literally, we must not forget the butterflies, birds and other nectar and pollen loving creatures that a well planned garden will attract.

Some bees are interested in more than just our flowers. The Leafcutter Bee (*Megachile* spp.) cuts neat semi-circular pieces out of soft leaves to build its unique nest, but who would begrudge her a few segments of rose leaf for this purpose. Providing artificial homes by drilling holes in timber blocks or bundling together short sections of bamboo or the like and securing them horizontally in sheltered areas may encourage Leafcutters, Resin Bees and some other species to take up permanent residence in your garden. Carpenter Bees, as their name implies, make the nests for their future offspring in pithy or decaying timber, but our Teddy Bear and Blue Banded Bees are more down to earth with their homemaking. They dig holes in the ground in sheltered places such as under Old Queenslander Houses that are elevated on stumps. Blue Banded Bees in particular will also nest in vertical earth walls and banks. They are known to build in the walls of rammed earth houses and may sometimes dig holes in the mortar between bricks if it happens to be soft enough. Artificial homes can be created for this species by making a low wall out of hollow concrete blocks filled with rammed earth or clay. Making a few decoy holes in the clay can also help to entice them to move in.

Left: This drilled hardwood block has been occupied by leafcutter bees in the top right section and by two mud wasps in the bottom left corner. Centre: Bamboo pieces placed in a sheltered location can entice a number of native bees to take up residence (photo courtesy Marc Newman) Right: These hollow concrete blocks filled with clay and drilled with decoy holes will hopefully be a Blue Banded Bee apartment block of the future.

But coming back to the garden plantings, some readers may be a little surprised to find that a publication of this nature does not exclusively promote the use of native plant species. While some of our solitary bees and particular native plants have evolved interdependence over time, this is not the case with our stingless social bees. Being diverse in their floral choices they are known as generalists. As such they were never likely to refuse the pollen and nectar rich blossoms that have been introduced in the brief period since Captain James Cook and Sir Joseph Banks visited their land and examined its plants.

In suburban situations, it is not uncommon to find stingless bees showing a preference for the 'exotics' over the native plant species. This was highlighted to me through a personal experience. Some years ago, I decided to upgrade my own garden to a bee friendly one to help feed all the artificial hives I have in my backyard. I visited a large garden nursery in a bushland setting and, grabbing one of their large wheeled trolleys, immediately headed off to the 'natives' section. As I passed the flowering Callistemons, Banksias, Melaleucas and Grevilleas I noticed several stingless bees in attendance, but their numbers paled by comparison with those visiting the exotics in the adjoining section.

When I finally pushed the trolley to the checkout it was loaded with a balance of both native and exotic flowering shrubs. I sought out plants that were not only attractive to the bees at the time, but also those that would provide an extended flowering period in the future. The staff members at the nursery were helpful and informative in this regard.

Left and centre: Grevilleas in all their forms and colours attract native bees, while Hakeas (right) are also sought after by foraging workers. (Photos on left and right courtesy Bob Luttrell)

Now you might be asking yourself 'what about the legendary nectar producing eucalypts and angophoras'? You would be right in suggesting that these (and some of our other larger forest trees) provide a rich source of stingless bee food (and commercial honey). However, most readers are likely to be living in an urban environment and, with a few exceptions, these trees are unsuitable for small allotments. If you have the space then certainly include them in your garden plantings - if not, you would be wise to confine yourself to the many shrubs of various sizes that are available.

With a careful selection of plants, your garden can be native bee friendly from the ground up. Flowering native ground covers combined with dwarf shrubs like the Baeckeas, can provide an understorey to the larger shrubs and small trees available from the range of callistemons, banksias, melaleucas and grevilleas. Native Cassias such as the Climbing Senna (*Senna gaudichaudii* or *S. surattensis*) produce a copious display of buttercup yellow flowers that are particularly attractive to our larger buzz pollinating bees. The leaves of these plants also feed the caterpillars of the Yellow Migrant butterfly (*Catopsilia gorgophone*), which enhances our garden with its own splash of moving colour in the warmer months.

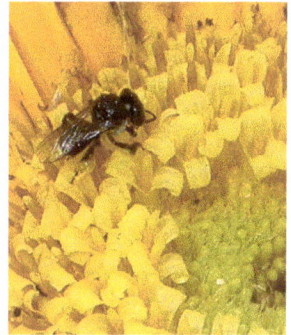

Old garden favourites such as this single white Camellia and the yellow Gerbera are a rich source of pollen for stingless bees.

If you are more multicultural in your horticultural pursuits, then there are of course a great number of foreign flowering plants to fill all the garden niches mentioned above. Most of the old time garden favourites will receive a visit if native bees are in the area, but there are some that will be totally ignored. The stingless bee magnets tend to be plants with open, accessible flowers with a high pollen content. Crepe Myrtle (*Lagerstroemia indica*) is popular with my bees and it seems to have a long flowering period. My bees also crowd into the single white blooms of my winter flowering Camellia, but don't go near the double pink variety with its convoluted blossoms. Similarly, the blaze of vivid white presented by the Snow Flake Bush (*Euphorbia leucocephala*) is totally ignored. It seems to possess neither pollen nor nectar in worthwhile quantities for them.

Sacred Bamboo is popular with stingless bees.

My wife's potted gerberas receive some interest from my bees, and the Crocus (*Zephyranthes* sp.) bulbs used as a garden edging produce pretty little pollen laden flowers that are a particular drawcard. Palms of all descriptions have been widely planted in my seaside suburb and the inflorescences they produce are popular with both honey bees and our stingless bees.

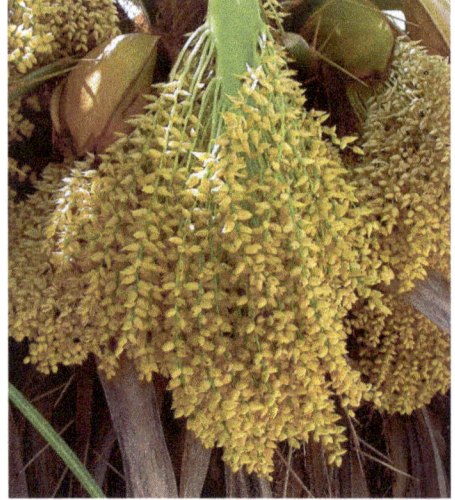

Palm trees sometimes produce large inflorescences which draw crowds of both honey bees and stingless bees. Presumably both of these social species, together with beetles and other insects, have contributed to the heavy seed set shown in the photo on the right.

On the plant side of the equation, it has to be said that stingless bees are not effective pollinators of all flowering plants. Many plants have specific pollination requirements and floral structures designed for other creatures. A stingless bee (or any other bee for that matter) may visit these flowers and leave fully loaded with pollen and nectar without fertilizing the stigma. Flowering plants have to tolerate many freeloaders, who take the rewards on offer without providing a service.

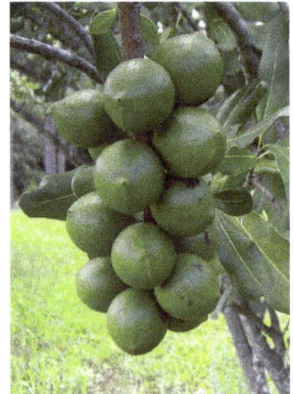

Stingless bees visit the flowers of many introduced food crops such as this strawberry blossom (left) but there is still a lot of work to be done to assess their effectiveness as pollinators. However, growers report that crops of our native macadamia nut are significantly improved when pollinated by Trigona bees (centre and right). (Left photo courtesy Carlos Alonso, right photo courtesy Frank Adcock.)

The interaction between flowering plants and Australia's social and solitary bees is an enormous and interesting field that the beekeeping botanists and keen gardeners might like to explore for themselves.

*Left: Paper Daisies make a colourful garden addition and are visited by native bees, such as this **Trigona carbonaria** worker. Including these plants in your garden also means you have a chance of breeding Australian Painted Lady butterflies (**Vanessa kershawi**). Centre: While Old Man's Saltbush, (**Atriplex nummularia**) makes an unusual inclusion in most coastal suburban gardens it attracts many forms of native bees when in flower. Right: Stingless bees are adaptable little creatures. In addition to collecting nectar from flowers they may also seek out other sugary secretions such as that exuded on the stems of wattles (in this case **Acacia bancrofti**). (Photos courtesy Bob Luttrell).*

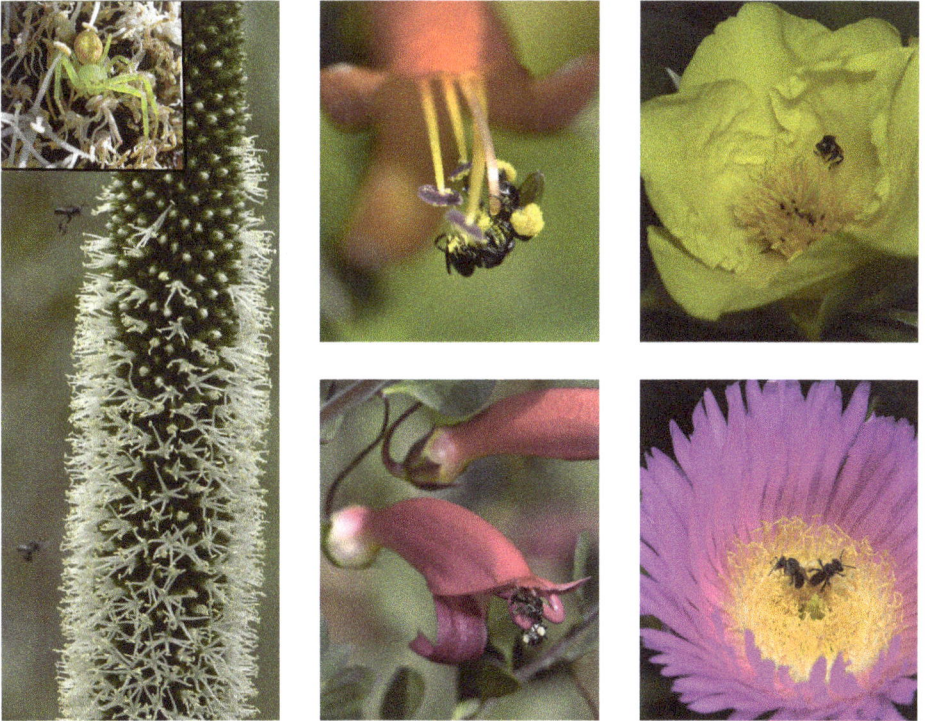

*Bob Luttrell has been exploring native bee and native plant interactions (photos courtesy Bob Luttrell) Left: Grass tree (**Xanthorrhoea** sp.) flower spikes provide a bountiful nectar source for stingless bees, but unfortunately sometimes danger lurks (inset spider).Stingless bee on **Eremophila** sp. (centre top), **Hibbertia** sp. (right top); Fraser Island Creeper (**Tecomanthe hillii**) (centre bottom), Pigface (**Carbrotus glaucescens**) (right bottom).*

A stingless bee at a muddy soak. It is likely she is seeking essential salts and minerals rather than the moisture itself. (Photo courtesy Bernhard Jacobi)

*Some Public Authorities are sensitive to the requirements of stingless bees. While trying to preserve this aging tree in Lesslie Park Warwick, Qld, council workers have also had regard for the old **Trigona carbonaria** colony in its base. The hive entrance is located between the chopped off trunk and one behind it.*

The Australian Native Bee Research Centre has published an award winning field guide for native bees of the Sydney region and at the time of writing another such guide, covering an extended area of Eastern Australia, is in production.

17. Mist in the Crystal Ball

The future of stingless beekeeping is difficult to predict. It may just remain as it is now – a minor hobby enjoyed by a few enthusiasts. However, signs are beginning to emerge that it may assume a more prominent role – and not just as a pastime.

The most obvious opportunity for stingless beekeepers is in the field of honey production. For some time now, people have been experimenting with special 'supers' to separate the honey pots from the brood and pollen storage areas in their hives. This not only makes harvesting easier but it also avoids damage to the brood and contamination with pollen that can adversely affect the flavour of the honey and cause fermentation. To coincide with this, there seems to be a niche market developing for sugarbag honey, especially in tourist areas. In the same market, cerumen is sold on a very limited scale for use in the manufacture of didgeridoos and other products of Aboriginal origin.

The medicinal properties of honey, especially stingless bee honey with its unique combination of chemicals infused from the resins in the cerumen honey pots, is another field to be explored. An increasing number of people are becoming convinced of the efficacy of this honey for treating a wide range of ailments. Certainly Aboriginal people believed it had healing powers. Pure stingless bees' wax can be obtained from the dark brown cerumen through the use of a solar wax extractor. Redolent with tree resins, it can be used in hand and body lotions or mixed with other waxes to produce fragrant candles.

A solar wax extractor can be used to obtain pure stingless bees wax from the brown cerumen. Redolent with the smell of tree resins, its full potential is yet to be explored but it may be suitable for aromatherapy and other alternative medicine therapies.

It is more likely, however, that stingless bees will make their real mark in the field of crop pollination. A small number of commercial stingless bee pollination services are up and running, and farmers using these bees report a measurable increase in their yield of crops such as macadamia nuts.

There is little doubt that honey bees are regarded as the world's foremost crop pollinator. In some countries providing bees to pollinate crops is big agricultural business, but it is not without its difficulties. Colony Collapse Disorder (CCD) is a major threat to commercial apiaries in some parts of the world and by extension to the food crops that rely upon these bees.

In some areas of Australia farmers rely on feral honey bees for pollinating a number of our food crops. These wild honey bees could be under serious threat in the future. The Small Hive Beetle has already reached our shores, and is also making its unwanted presence felt. On its own it has the potential to decimate feral honey bee colonies but, if the even more

Mark and Kim Grosskopf live on Queensland's Darling Downs and provide a commercial pollination service using Australian Stingless Bees. At the time this photograph was taken Kim was expecting their son, Kerry, who hopefully will follow in their footsteps to be a stingless beekeeper of the future.

Well-insulated hives fitted with low voltage artificial heating devices, such as the one shown, may prove to be the answer to keeping stingless bees in colder areas of Australia.

devastating Varoa mite also crosses our quarantine barriers, the effect on crops dependent on these bees could be very significant indeed.

Stingless bees have the potential to step into the breach if they are properly housed and managed. There is no denying they have some shortcomings, not the least being their limited natural range which restricts them to the tropical, sub-tropical and warm temperate areas of our country. However, several stingless beekeepers are experimenting with things such as heavily insulated hives, supplementary feeding and even artificial heating.

A lot of research and development has to be done in these areas before we can determine the likelihood of our stingless bees not only surviving a southern winter with this assistance, but also emerging in spring in sufficient numbers to be effective pollinators of early crops.

Of equal importance in a commercial setting would be the need to look at breeding to improve the stock by concentrating on strains with desirable characteristics. Our stinging bee colleagues recognized the benefits of controlled queen raising a long time ago, and we may

Bob Raymond of Miles has a large collection of stingless bees and is experimenting with different propagation methods and queen rearing.

need to explore the potential of adopting equivalent practices for our native social bees in artificial hives. We may have to stop short of the artificial insemination techniques they also employ, but who knows. It is such an open field there is great scope for experimentation.

Even if turns out that Australian farmers do not show much interest in our little home grown pollinators, such may not be the case overseas. The Japanese have already conducted trials of our Trigona bees for greenhouse pollination and Israel has also shown considerable interest in obtaining our stingless bees for outdoor pollination duties. Should these projects prove fruitful, then no doubt the interest in stingless beekeeping will reach new heights. One might say the sky is the limit, by why stop there. In August 2007 the Australian Newspaper ran a prominent article outlining how Australian school children in Melbourne are assisting a

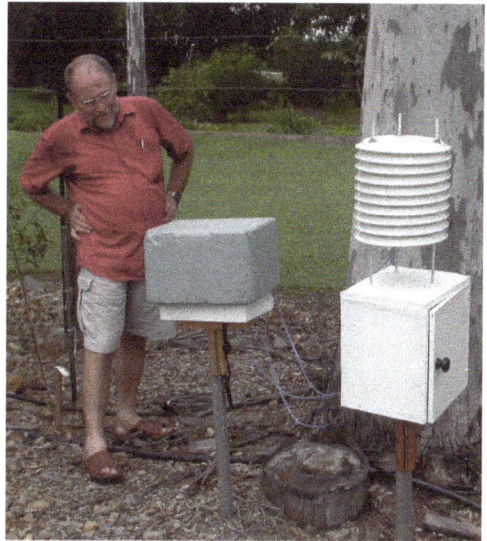

Bob Luttrell's interest in native bees is not confined to taking fine photographs. Here he is shown inspecting one of his hives that is fitted with equipment to measure temperature fluctuations which can then be downloaded for computer analysis.

scientist to assess the possibility of using Trigona bees to pollinate food crops in space stations. This probably only confirms what a lot of stingless beekeepers already know – that such a hobby is out of this world.

Glossary

Advancing Front: The area of the brood comb where the latest brood cells have been constructed.

Batumen: A thick layer of hard cerumen, often incorporating various other materials, that encloses and protects the entire nest cavity of stingless bees.

Brood, Brood Comb, Brood Mass: Collective terms for young developing bees in the egg, larval and pupa state.

Brood Cell: The individual cerumen capsule constructed by stingless bees in which the egg is laid and the young bee develops.

Callow: A young, but fully developed bee that has recently emerged from its brood cell. Callows are noticeably lighter in colour than older bees.

Cerumen: The brown building material used by stingless bees consisting of a mixture of wax, secreted by young bees, and tree resins collected by the foragers.

Cocoon: A casing of silk spun within the brood cell by the stingless bee larvae immediately prior to pupation.

Compound Eyes: The external surface of the insect eye comprised of numerous (in some cases many thousand) individual facets enabling a large angle of view but lacking high image resolution.

Corbicula: (pl. Corbiculae)
The modified tibia of the hind legs of stingless bees (and some other bee species) used to secure and transport pollen. Usually referred to as the 'pollen basket'.

Flagellum: In bees, the extended whip like part of the antenna, typically comprised of 10 - 11 segments.

Hive, Colony & Nest: These terms have been employed without rigorous distinction in line with everyday general usage. However, in the main 'Colony' and 'Nest' refer to the bees and their brood collectively, whereas 'Hive' has been used to describe the enclosure for housing bees (including the colony within - when occupied) regardless of whether this is an artificial structure such as a box or a natural feature such as a hollow tree.

Imago: The final (adult) stage of the bee's development.

Involucrum: An insulating sheath of thin cerumen (often multi-layered) enclosing the brood area of the hive.

Larva: (pl. Larvae)
The second stage in a bee's development; the 'worm' or 'grub' stage.

Mandibles: The jaws. In bees (and most other insects) the mandibles move horizontally rather than vertically as they do in mammals and reptiles.

Parthenogenesis: Reproduction by means of unfertilised eggs. In bees only males (drones) develop from unfertilised eggs.

Pedicel: The second segment of a bee's antenna, between the scape and the flagellum.

Pheromones: Chemical messenger substances secreted by bees (and many other organisms) which trigger particular behavioural responses in other members of the same species.

Propolis: A (usually) dark coloured resin collected and used by honey bees to seal up cracks and to secure hive components. Sometimes referred to as 'Bee Glue'.

Pupa: (pl. Pupae)
The third stage (following the egg and larval stages) of a bee's development, during which it is inactive within its cocoon. During the time of pupation the larval structures are broken down to reform as the adult insect.

Queen Cell: A brood cell constructed to house developing queen bees. It is considerably larger (up to 4 times the volume) of a worker brood cell.

Scape: The basal segment of a bee's antenna (closest to the face). In our stingless bees the scape is long and straight.

Spermatheca: A sac forming part of the queen bee's reproductive tract in which are stored the spermatozoa from the drone with which she mated.

Stigma: The pollen receptor within a flower.

Super: A receptacle associated with artificial hives, usually in the form of an extension or additional section, in which bees can store excess honey.

Register of Stingless Beehives in Public Places

Location & Description of hive (including the most likely type of bee)	GPS Coordinates
Dee Why NSW – on display in Stoney Range Nature Reserve. Believed to be over 20 yrs old. *Trigona carbonaria*	
Monto Qld – in old Ironbark stump in front grounds of Monto Hospital. Stump capped with concrete paver. *Trigona carbonaria*	
Brisbane Qld, Buckley St Carina - in public reserve near creek. In old stump (possibly Casuarina) capped with piece of roofing iron. *Trigona carbonaria*	S 27° 30.532' E 153° 05.647'
Brisbane Qld, Park Ave, East Brisbane – 2 nests both approx 3m high in Camphor Laurel tree on footpath adjacent to vehicle entrance to East Bne Bowls Club. *Trigona carbonaria*	S 27° 28.718' E 153° 02.553'
Brisbane Qld, Park Ave, East Brisbane (opposite intersection with Thorn St) – very low down in footpath tree near entrance to Mowbray Park parking area. *Trigona carbonaria*	S 27° 28.684' E 153° 02.564'
Cecil Plains area, Qld – eye level in roadside Gum tree. *Trigona carbonaria*	S 27° 36.375' E 151° 07.698'
Tara/Dalby area, Qld – in roadside tree, Moonie Hwy. *Austroplebeia australis*	S 27° 15.546' E 151° 04.739'
Tara/Dalby area, Qld – in roadside tree, Moonie Hwy. *Austroplebeia australis*	S 27° 15.581' E 151° 04.662'
Warwick Qld – low in old ornamental tree just inside Leslie Park on Guy St side. *Trigona carbonaria*	S 28° 12.760' E 152° 01.867'
Gleneagle (near Beaudesert) SE Qld – low down in roadside tree (possibly Small Leaf Box) near entrance to Captain Logan Memorial site, Mt Lindsay Hwy (Beaudesert Rd). *Trigona carbonaria*	S 27° 57.185' E 152° 59.147'
Capalaba (East of Brisbane) SE Qld – high in large (living) Tallowwood in reserve on Eastern side of Redland Bay Rd. *Trigona carbonaria*	S 27° 32.352' E 153° 12.937'
Capalaba (East of Brisbane) SE Qld – high in large (living) Tallowwood in reserve on Eastern side of Redland Bay Rd. *Trigona carbonaria*	S 27° 32.332' E 153° 12.943'
Cleveland SE Qld – 1.6 metres above ground in living paperbark tree in park behind primary school. Tree located approximately 10 metres from concrete path near easternmost pedestrian bridge in park – *Trigona carbonaria*	S 27° 31.772' E 153° 16.374'
Capalaba (East of Brisbane) SE Qld – approx 4 metres up a standing dead tree near walking track in reserve on Eastern side of Redland Bay Rd. Approx 50 metres North of viewing platform on track - *Trigona carbonaria*	S 27° 32.365' E 153° 12.917'
Cooktown NQ – in Captain Cook memorial at the waterfront end of Charlotte St. Bees emerge from one of the animal heads previously used as water fountains. Believed to have occupied this site since before 1963.	
Teneriffe (Inner Brisbane) SE Qld - in the base of a large Moreton Bay fig (western side of tree) that is in Teneriffe Park near New Farm (little park on the top of Teneriffe Hill). Believed to have occupied this site for approx 13 years – *Trigona carbonaria*	
Roma Street Parkland (Inner Brisbane Park) SE Qld - in the base of a fig tree (third one of a series of four) in garden just outside entrance of Spectacle Garden as you enter from Albert Park – *Trigona carbonaria*	

Yeronga (Brisbane) - there are three hives in two Tallowood trees in Yeronga Park close to the Yeronga Meals on Wheels in School Road. One (A) shares a tree with an Apis hive. The other two are located in a nearby tree, one in the area of a rotted out root (B), the other (C) about 2.5 metres up the tree on the eastern side – all three appear to be *Trigona carbonaria*	(A) S 27° 31.289' E 153° 01.451' (B) & (C) S 27° 31.285' E 153° 01.444'
Yeronga (Brisbane) – approximately 6 metres above the ground in a major branch of a Tallowood tree in Yeronga Park. The tree housing this hive is quite close to the two Tallowoods mentioned in the entry immediately above – *Trigona carbonaria*	S 27° 31.272' E 153° 01.455'
Yeronga (Brisbane) - in a spotted gum near the Yeronga State Preschool located on the fence line between Yeronga Park and the Preschool, School Road – *Trigona carbonaria*	S 27° 31.183' E 153° 01.302'
Dutton Park (Brisbane) – in a Moreton Bay Fig tree within the parkland itself, close to the tight curve in the old pathway to the cross river ferry to Qld university – *Trigona carbonaria*	
Yeronga (Brisbane) – in a Bloodwood tree on the footpath on Honour Ave (which enters the park from the Park Rd side) between the tennis courts and the gate to Yeronga Primary School. Hive is about 7 feet up on the eastern side of the tree – *Trigona carbonaria*	S 27° 31.101' E 153° 01.235'
Wellington Point, SE Qld – on South Western side of a large tree on footpath outside number 294, Main Road – *Trigona carbonaria*	S 27° 28.873' E 153° 14.297'
New Farm (inner Brisbane) – in Camphor Laurel tree on footpath outside number 34, Abbott Street – *Trigona carbonaria*	
New Farm (inner Brisbane) – in Camphor Laurel tree on footpath outside number 37, Abbott Street – *Trigona carbonaria*	
New Farm (inner Brisbane) – in Camphor Laurel tree on footpath outside number 15, Abbott Street – *Trigona carbonaria*	
New Farm (inner Brisbane) – in Camphor Laurel tree on footpath outside number 22, Abbott Street – *Trigona carbonaria*	
New Farm (inner Brisbane) – two hives (and a honeybee colony) in Camphor Laurel tree on footpath outside units at number 14, Abbott Street – *Trigona carbonaria*	
New Farm (inner Brisbane) – on topside of a low branch of a Camphor Laurel tree on footpath outside number 1, Abbott Street (second tree along) – *Trigona carbonaria*	
New Farm (inner Brisbane) – in Camphor Laurel tree on footpath outside number 49, Sydney Street – Trigona carbonaria New Farm (inner Brisbane) – in Camphor Laurel tree on footpath outside number 55, Sydney Street – *Trigona carbonaria*	
Ma Ma Creek SE Qld – in Iron Bark tree on road verge outside State School & Anglican Church grounds – *Trigona carbonaria*	S 27° 37.753' E 152° 11.362'
Cairns Botanical Gardens Nth Qld – in the wall facing you as you climb the steps to the Office, high up near the roof. Believed to be at least 15 years old	
Port Douglas Nth Qld – in timber at the entrance to the little white church near the jetty.	
Sydney NSW – behind the kiosk in the Animal/Bird sanctuary at Lane Cove River National Park – *Trigona carbonaria*	

North Parramatta, Sydney NSW – in Lake Parramatta Reserve approximately 200 metres along the walking track that begins at the end of the car park inside the Lackey Street entrance. Hive is knee hive in a gum tree right beside the track where there is a bend in the lake. Hive entrance faces away from car park – *Trigona carbonaria*

St Lucia (Brisbane) – in Poinciana tree on footpath outside 26 Laurence St. – *Trigona carbonaria*

St Lucia (Brisbane) – in Camphor Laurel tree within the 'soft fall' area of children's playground situated at the end of Hiron Street – *Trigona carbonaria*

Dutton Park (Brisbane) – two hives in the one Cypress Pine tree in Dutton Park cemetery, about 20 metres up from the intersection of Princess St and Fairfield Rd and facing into Fairfield Rd – *Trigona carbonaria*

Chelmer (Brisbane) – low down on roadside of Camphor Laurel tree on footpath near the border of nos. 14 & 16 Laurel Ave – *Trigona carbonaria*

Chelmer (Brisbane) – in Camphor Laurel branch overhanging road & facing east on footpath outside no. 128 Laurel Ave – *Trigona carbonaria*

Dutton Park (Brisbane) – two hives in large stumps located within small area of bush garden located close to Gladstone Rd, near to dog 'off leash' area – *Trigona carbonaria*

West End (Brisbane) – 4 metres high on southern side of Camphor Laurel treein Boundary St near intersection with Montague Rd (near Paul's weighbridge) – *Trigona carbonaria*

Contacts & Resources

ANBees Yahoo! Chat Group:http://pets.groups.yahoo.com/group/ANBees/ is an active forum for discussions on all sorts of Australian native bee topics.

ANBees Website: http://www.australiannativebees.com/ is a website compiled by the members of the ANBees Yahoo! chat group, with articles, photos and information about Australian native bees.

Australian Native Bees Research Centre (ANBRC): www.aussiebee.com.au
Dr Anne Dollin provides information and photographs on native bees plus a range of booklets: -

- **Introduction to Australian Native Bees** covering: Solitary, semi-social and social stingless bees; Where stingless bees live; Stingless bee nests; Stingless bees & the garden

- **Nests of Australian Stingless Bees** covering: The entrance; Honey and pollen pots; The nest cavity; The brood; Nest materials; The batumen

- **Behaviour of Australian Stingless Bees** covering: The castes; Waste disposal; Life cycle; Nest defence; Brood construction; Foraging; Temperature control

- **How to Recognise the Different Types of Australian Stingless Bee** covering: social stingless bees only; Native bee anatomy; Species Identification; The workers, Drones and queens

- **Keeping Australian Stingless Bees in a Log or Box** by Dr Anne Dollin ANBRC & Dr Tim Heard CSIRO covering: The basic methods; Box design; Boxing nests; Splitting nests; Harvesting honey; Nest maintenance

- **Crop Pollination with Australian Stingless Bees** by Dr Tim Heard CSIRO & Dr Anne Dollin ANBRC covering: Should We Use Native Bees Commercially; Pros and Cons of Stingless Bees for Crop Pollination; Detailed Survey of Suitable Crops; Managing Stingless Bee Hives for Crop Pollination

- **Tips on Stingless Beekeeping by Australian Beekeepers – Volume 1** Tips from 30 Australian beekeepers and the 1999 Survey Results, compiled by Dr Anne Dollin ANBRC & Dr Tim Heard CSIRO covering: Box designs; Transferring nests; Splitting nests; Siting hives; Hive insulation; Supplementary feeding; Honey harvesting; Warnings

- **Tips on Stingless Beekeeping by Australian Beekeepers – Volume 2** containing tips from over 120 Australian beekeepers in the 2000 Survey, covering: Finding nests; Siting hives; Hive boxes in current use; Insulating hives; Avoiding overheating; New box designs; Experimental heated hives; Harvesting honey

- **Tips on Stingless Beekeeping by Australian Beekeepers – Volume 3** comprising more tips from Australian beekeepers in the 2000 Survey, covering: Strengthening hives; Predator control; Torelliana resin; Fighting swarms; Crop pollination; Preventing hive theft; Breeding queen bees; Avoiding hive deaths

- **Boxing and Splitting Hives:** A Full Do-It Yourself Guide by Dr Anne Dollin ANBRC and Russell and Janine Zabel with a full colour cover and over 70 photographs and drawings, covering: Rescuing a nest from the bush; Boxing a nest; Transferring a large nest into two boxes; Splitting hives; Troubleshooting guide

Australian Stingless Native Bees: http://www.zabel.com.au comprises abundant stories, photos and fact sheets on stingless native bees by Russell and Janine Zabel. Services include: Trigona carbonaria and Austroplebeia australis nest sales, boxing and nest rescue.

Sugarbag: Honey and Wax from Stingless Bees: http://www.sugarbag.net by Dr Tim Heard includes photos and inform-ation about stingless bees and their honey (sugarbag) and waxes (cerumen). Services include hive sales and beekeeping resources.

Index

www.ingramcontent.com/pod-product-compliance
Lightning Source LLC
Chambersburg PA
CBHW041259040426
42334CB00028BA/3088